D1592744

9336262

ICARUS 2.0

PARACHUTE INCLUDED

A Father's InCentivE$ for CREATEing Our Way

Peter Smith

Copyright © Peter Smith

"The views expressed in this publication are those of the authors and contributors and do not necessarily reflect the official policy or position of the Department of Defense or the U.S. Government."

Print ISBN: 978-1-09839-994-8
eBook ISBN: 978-1-09839-995-5

For Erika, Dean, Cole, and Jessica
"More than the whole universe"
"Infinite"
"Never ends"

*Dedicated to future leaders and educators inspiring worldly self-actualiza-
tion while ensuring that our nation remains a constitutional republic.*

CONTENTS

LIST OF FIGURES

FOREWORD

Surviving an ejection at over 400 mph can affect your outlook. Probably fewer than fifty pilots worldwide have made it through that kind of a beating. The night Pete punched out was perhaps as emotional for me as him. I went from screaming into my oxygen mask, enraged that his beautiful family had lost him, to immense and total joy at his tired-sounding, scratchy post-ejection radio transmission: "Mayday, Mayday, Mayday, Shark 22, I'm in the water, I'm OK."

The art and science of raising our children to be good citizens and good persons is an ever-changing skill. The way our parents raised us doesn't look much like us raising our own children today—and the pace of that change seems to be increasing.

This guidebook, or checklist, if you like, is an invaluable aid to families. It invites families to face the challenge of creating good citizens and good people and not just to cope with it, but to solve it with a positive outcome.

Pete was given a second chance at life when he survived a high-speed ejection into a rough, cold ocean at night. With *Icarus 2.0*, he gives back, in spades. Good hunting!

Courtney "Rosco" Collier
Colonel, USAFR
93rd Fighter Squadron "Makos"

PART 1:

Blue Side Up?

PROLOGUE:

My Accident

In Greek mythology, Icarus and his father, Daedalus, escape from King Minotaur's Isle of Crete, using wings made by Daedalus. Despite his father's warnings, Icarus is killed when he flies too high and too close to the sun, melting the wax and burning the feathers attached to his wings. He falls into the sea and drowns.

"Mayday, Mayday, Mayday, Shark 22, I'm in the water, I'm OK." January 15, 2008, started out routinely. My wife and I got the kids up, enjoyed breakfast together, and walked them to school. We returned home, put our littlest one in the car, and headed to our local gym. Once we finished our workouts, we grabbed a couple tuna sandwiches at our favorite lunch spot before returning home so I could get ready for work. That day's mission was Red Air. Our job was to disrupt and destroy Blue Air's game plan, preventing them from successfully reaching their target. I was a wingman, which meant I was in a support role for my flight lead. I only needed to assist with the weather, Notices to Airman (NOTAM), threats, and the emergency procedure of the day. Since I didn't have to coordinate and develop the entire tactical game plans of both sorties, I could focus on improving my defensive tactics. We were flying twice that day as Red Air—a daytime mission, followed by a turnaround for a similar Red Air sortie at night. I had decided my personal desired learning objective (DLO) would be executing and evaluating a text-book defensive maneuver. This maneuver is aggressive in execution, with many risk factors to consider. My thought process was that because so much of our tactical flying was shifting to night operations—and I didn't want my first time executing the maneuver to be in combat, at night, over the Taiwan Strait—I may as well practice during the day sortie and then polish the maneuver at night.

Our daytime sortie went well, but I made some mistakes executing the tactic by the book, which negated the effectiveness of the maneuver. I planned to clean up my mistakes that night, if my flight lead's tactics allowed. The forecast for our night mission over the Gulf of Mexico included low clouds over the water, unlimited visibility, and a bright moon for Night Vision Goggles (NVGs). Initially, my flight lead's tactics did not call for me to exercise my tactical intention; however, Blue Air was delayed coming off the air refueling tanker, while we burned down mission-critical fuel holding in our Combat Air Patrol (CAP). The Blue Air Mission Commander of the four-ship formation would "push" late to meet their Time over Target (TOT). This is where the holes in my "Swiss cheese"—as we pilots say—began lining up.

The Swiss cheese model for accident prevention (Figure 1) is something pilots are quite familiar with. The concept is to set up traps such as checklists, operational risk management (ORM) procedures, use of tactical decision aides, wingman input and consideration, proficiency, and reduction of mission complexity to prevent or offset cumulative errors (holes) from aligning all the way through the Swiss cheese to the other side, all representing a mishap or accident.

6

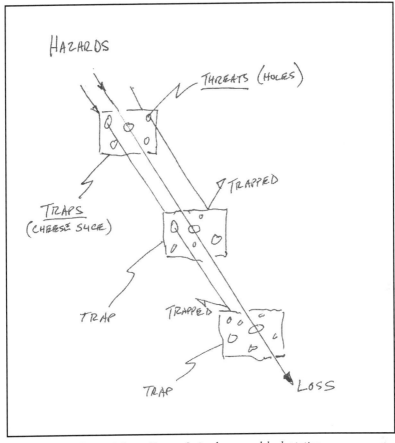

Figure 1. James Reason Swiss cheese model adaptation.

The holes in my Swiss cheese were beginning to align as we stepped up to our clean F-16s for our evening mission. Because Blue Air was behind their timeline, we would have to modify our original game plan in order to conserve fuel and still provide them adequate training. Originally, my flight lead's Red Air game plan would not have allowed me to execute the tactic I intended to practice on my own. Now that Blue Air was late for their "Push" to the target, however, my flight lead, Shark 21, modified the plan to provide enough training to meet Blue Air's objectives. This modification allowed me to reconsider executing my tactic as intended. We were established in our CAP, on time, in super-clean F-16s. We had no wingtip missiles or external wing fuel tank drag, and much lower fuel quantity than the Blue Air configured jets we were fighting. This is not how we usually trained as Red Air for this mission (the first hole in my Swiss cheese). Normally we were configured the same as Blue Air, according to the mission tactical phase of training being executed for the month. But due to training requirements and maintenance, the aircraft we took off in were cleanly configured F-16s. A clean F-16 is a highly maneuverable, low-drag, high-speed scream machine carrying less fuel than the Blue Air jets configured with external wing tanks we were fighting against. A cleanly configured jet was beneficial tactically for executing my objective. However, I hadn't considered the increased performance threat (another hole) for my first attempt at this defensive maneuver, at night, in a clean F-16 rather than my more familiar tanked-up, draggy jet. I had not set a trap in consideration of my inexperience executing the maneuver at night. Choosing a less aggressive maneuver with respect to the dangerous environment I was flying would have been appropriate.

Air combat tactics conducted above the water and at night make for unforgivable maneuvering environments. These require proficiency, confidence, fully functional instrumentation, properly illuminated avionics, a discernible horizon, and cultural lighting—if you can get it. We are trained not to complacently turn night into day under the aid of our NVGs. I felt confident continuing my personal training objective, given the above factors. However, I was unintentionally creating a perfect storm for "spatial disorientation."

My flight lead modified our game plan allowing me to exercise my tactic. When Blue Air "pushed" from their starting point, we had enough fuel to provide a less complicated ingress "picture" for them to tackle, conserving enough fuel for an enemy egress "picture" while servicing their targets. Our goal was to give Blue Air a problem to solve on and off target prior to reaching "Bingo" fuel and having to RTB (Return to Base).

Considering the excellent moon illumination for NVGs, our perceived discernible horizon, and my comfort level with the environmental conditions, I decided to execute the maneuver. I chose to turn toward the dark abyss over the Gulf of Mexico, littered with illuminated shrimping boats (stars), and a lower strip layer of cirrus clouds (false horizon visual illusion). It would have been wiser to turn toward the cultural lighting off the coast, to help trap any of the spatial disorientation effects of the aggressive maneuvering. I thought I had executed the maneuver well, until I began hearing the distinct familiar auditory hum of an F-16 canopy approaching 1.0 Mach. "Why am I going so fast?" The picture and attitude my brain was perceiving visually appeared to be a familiar 30-degree nose low attitude, wings banked level with the horizon. I believe (we'll never really know) I transferred my horizon to the moonlit thin cirrus layer of clouds just above the ocean floor while aggressively turning and descending simultaneously. The ocean now became my sky, and the straight edge of the cirrus cloud layer became my horizon reference. I didn't recognize it through my NVGs. "I shouldn't be going so fast with the power at idle, right?" I thought. Instinctively, I began pulling back on the stick to slow down as my cross-check was currently inside the cockpit. I was rapidly descending into my safety block of airspace. When I looked back outside the horizon picture I had referenced just seconds before had disappeared into a pure-black, zero-contrast picture outside my canopy. "Strange," I thought. "Did I enter clouds?" I cross-checked my altitude in the Heads-Up Display (HUD) as I was passing 18,000 feet. I needed to continue my descent into my assigned airspace block of 10,000 to 14,000 feet. I assumed I had enough time to figure out what was going on while descending. Since I had a few seconds before entering my airspace, I rotated my head to the right side of the canopy in search of my last known visual references and cultural lighting cues for the horizon. "Nothing...What's going on here?" Again, I thought, "I'll figure it out in my block." The visual illusion, coupled with my vestibular sensations and probable vertigo while maneuvering, had tricked me into an unintended inverted roll. I didn't see the cultural lighting picture I'd expected, because I was probably staring at the ocean below, now imperceptibly upside down. I didn't notice that my aircraft attitude was inverted, since everything seemed normal visually except for my recent loss of the horizon. The auditory cues made me suspicious something was not quite right, but I needed to wait until safely in my assigned block of airspace to address the suspicion. The holes were lining up, as I continued descending despite the audible high-speed cue warning me of my current unusual attitude. I initiated level-off just passing 14,000 feet. "That didn't feel right," I thought. It felt like I accelerated, and that sound of high-speed humming resonating outside the canopy became louder as I noticed through the HUD my rate of altitude loss accelerating. "Ok, I'm disoriented—get on the round dial gauges: "Recognize, Confirm, Recover!" I was now descending toward the water at an approximate rate of 1,000 feet per second. I immediately snapped my cross-check to the center pedestal instruments (round dial gauges) to see myself passing 9,700 feet, altimeter winding down counterclockwise at an alarming rate, with my airspeed approaching 600 knots and only a dot on the top of my attitude indicator (ADI) visible. *Recognition* of spatial disorientation was complete. *Confirmation* of spatial disorientation was complete. Time to *recover*! That was all I had left. I couldn't see any horizon lines to reference on the ADI. "Which way do I point the tail?" My nose was buried almost vertically, straight down at high speed, as I stared at a black dot tumbling on the ADI. I had exceeded the instrument's nose low reference limits and failed to incorporate the ADI's perimeter sky pointer reference into my instrument cross-check at this moment (Why? I simply hadn't trained enough using the small sky pointer reference on our ADI to recover from unusual attitudes—and now my life depended on it. Another hole in my Swiss cheese). My first thought was, "I'm pointed straight down, too fast to eject, with no idea which way my wings are in relation to the horizon in order to orient the tail in the quickest correct direction to pull up. I have to guess my pull into the ADI wing reference and horizon lines." I immediately input a maximum g limiter (approximately 9 g's, nine times the force of gravity) pull to get my ADI aircraft symbol back to the horizon reference lines and slow the jet down. Speed-brakes extended, and stick pulled back, I hoped it would be the shortest direction to the horizon with a straight, no-bank-angle pull as I strained against the g-forces. I was keeping up with the altimeter's alarmingly unsettling rapid counterclockwise winddown—8,000 . . . 7,000 . . . 6,000 (uncontrolled bailout altitude)—and as the

ADI spun and wobbled into lines, my brain wasn't able to process fast enough. We're supposed to eject the aircraft at 6,000 feet above ground level when out of control, but I was close to 500 knots and too fast to eject without risk of serious injury or death from flailing injuries ejecting into the 575 mph apparent wind force against my body. I had to wait and slow the aircraft down. As I was passing 6,000 feet, my NVGs started filling up with ambient light, illuminating outside visual references again as I descended into the low-level cloud layer reflecting off the moonlight. "Maybe I can catch the horizon?" I decided to transfer my internal visual cross-check outside the canopy to look for the horizon trading valuable milliseconds not interpreting my instruments for hope of outside visual cues. I made the decision to look outside, approaching 5,000 feet and 400 knots, knowing that the quickest way to straighten out my brain in my short amount of time remaining was to see the natural horizon outside, instinctively helping me visually correct my attitude in relation to it. Unfortunately, I couldn't see the horizon outside in those milliseconds. Only clouds, moonlight reflections and lighter/darker contrasts creating a "milk bowl" visual effect with no discernible horizon. I came back to my aircraft symbol on the ADI, cross-checking my instruments, now verifying definite right roll (a death spiral similar to what killed JFK Jr.), against the brown down attitude indicator horizon reference lines passing 4500 feet and just below 400 knots. I snapped the stick to the left to slow the roll but couldn't mentally process the aircraft reference symbol against the ADI background. My aircraft's rate of descent was draining all of my processing power as I rapidly approached mandatory ejection, 2,000 feet above the sea. This was all happening fast. Imagine your brain is plugging along, operating at a 186-chip processing speed but is then suddenly upgraded to a Pentium processor. Adrenaline and endorphins were surging through my body and brain. My brain was lit up trying to solve the problem at the same time the near-death movie reel played in the background. I made a last ditch attempt passing 4000 feet thinking I could deliberately unload and push the stick forward to slow the descent rate momentarily freezing the attitude picture on my ADI, then reload stick aft to see what happens. "Rate slows;

I'm blue side up. Rate accelerates; I'm upside down.", I thought. A futile attempt abandoned abruptly around 2500 feet as my altimeter rapidly unwound the available altitude my last ditch roll, pull and afterburner input needed to recover. I made the decision to—"Eject, Eject, Eject!"—2,000—my hands came off the stick and throttle, thumbs thrust deliberately into the ejection handle loops. I pulled. Nothing happened. "I waited too long!" Time seemed to temporally distort in my mind and slow down. I became hyper-aware, anticipating impact with the water. My breathing slowed as if it were my last and body relaxed. I felt like Neo in the *The Matrix*, when he dodges bullets in slow motion. "Why is this seat not going up the rails?" I looked down and to the left. "Did I forget to arm the seat?" I wondered. "No, it's armed." I thought, "I can't believe I made it this far and the seat is broken." The last altitude I saw was just over 1,300 feet on the altimeter and approximately 350 knots as I started to reach for the alternate canopy ejection handle. I now suspected a canopy seat sequence malfunction. The alternate canopy ejection handle allows a pilot to manually blow the canopy so the seat will then initiate ejection. The canopy has to go first in the sequence. About this same time and before I could reach for the yellow canopy ejection handle, I began hearing loud pops. The cockpit filled with orange light, obscuring my instruments. The noise was briefly incredibly loud, followed by massive pressure against my chest. The air was pushed from my lungs knocking the wind out of me. My neck twisted fully to the right, with my head back and body stretched out contorting to the left. My mind had already begun to transition, expecting certain death, so everything felt dreamy and surreal. "This isn't so bad," I thought. "Dying is kind of peaceful." A brief flash of light exposed what appeared to be four quadrants of my parachute opening. "Is that my parachute?" The violence ceased abruptly, but I still felt conscious in an eerie, dreamy, pitch-black silence. The cloud layer above blocked any moonlight. My night vision goggles had been ripped off during the ejection. There was no ambient light, just darkness. "I kind of feel like . . . I'm still alive . . . ?" I sent a message to my arms and fingers to pinch the skin under my harness near my armpits. I squeezed my thumb and the side of my index finger down hard on my flight suit. "Hey, I felt that. Holy shit, I'm alive!" "Canopy, visor" . . . Splash! I entered the water.

I couldn't believe how fast things went wrong and how helpless I felt trying to solve the disorientation I experienced. "I just crashed a perfectly good airplane. This is gonna be hard to get over", I thought. Bobbing around in my one-man raft to the will of the wind and waves while blindly feeling around for specific survival gear to facilitate my rescue, I couldn't help thinking back to my first real experience with flying, after expressing interest when I was around 15 years old. My father, an airline pilot at the time, took me out in a rented Cessna 152 to teach me. While flying along, he would sometimes put the aircraft into a spin, fold his arms and tell me to recover, unknowingly initiating years of training and conditioning to think procedurally beyond the "startle effect." In my junior year at the United States Air Force Academy, Dad bought my graduation ring and had it inscribed, *"Blue Side Up-Dad"*. I couldn't help thinking about how badly I had just failed to heed my father's warning as I paddled around in the cool, wintry, windy sea states of the Gulf of Mexico, while firing off flares and talking back and forth to my wingmen on the radio. I had failed to keep the blue side up, despite 27 years of flying experience and almost 3,000 hours in fighter and attack aircraft.

A little over nine seconds had passed from the moment I confirmed my spatial disorientation to the moment I made the decision to eject. The engineers who analyzed and reviewed my aircraft's black box data calculated that I had less than a second left to live before I would have exited the ejection envelope and fatally impacted the water.

I was lucky. I was grateful for my wingmen and all personnel who spent the next hour and 40 minutes orchestrating my rescue. It would take me a while to thank everyone in the human chain who helped save my life. I got to many of them individually, but it would take a lifetime to thank them all.

Unlike Daedalus—mostly isolated, held captive on the Isle of Crete—I was fortunate to be connected to the collective of human ingenuity. I was grateful for my fellow Americans' technological genius and attention to detail in the design, manufacture, and maintenance of the ACES II ejection seat. I'm grateful to my mentors, instructors, colleagues, and leaders. They taught us and ensured that we were trained to be lethal in our weapon system and think things through procedurally. I was familiar with my human limits in our arena. When all efforts failed to save the jet, I knew to save myself and, as we say in our business, "give the jet back to the taxpayers." Without so many humans caring for and risking their own lives to save mine, I too would have gone the way of Icarus.

INTRODUCTION

Shortly after my accident, I sat down to write lessons I'd learned, for my children to consider should they move into adulthood without me. *Incentives* was a great word to frame my advice, as the definition is understood to represent things motivating or encouraging us to do something with our lives. I created an acronym containing three of what I consider the key virtues and seven (or so) habits to practice as my children navigate uncertainty, doubt, and imperfection in their lives.

I wrote the lessons down. I didn't preach or have any particular expectations. I simply tried to exemplify what I wrote and then get on with the task of raising my kids with my wife. It wasn't until their launch from high school that I was inspired to revisit the lessons and take them a little further by building an online blog and mentoring resource for students to reference. My wife and I now had some experience launching adolescents in our new normal of smartphone and 24/7 social media distractions—all this in addition to guidance counseling programs challenged by budgets, relevance, and time. There was a lot of distraction, doubt, uncertainty, and imperfect thinking regarding their options, and not many people besides their parents able to walk them through these obstacles. When COVID-19 hit in 2020, I knew it wasn't going to get any easier for our kids to receive face-to-face mentoring or guidance, so I put together a website combating limiting thoughts while explaining various nonstandard options available after high school in higher education, scholarships, skills, trades, military, ROTC, and service academies. I continue to be intent on collecting data and comments from "been there, done that" mentoring resources willing to share their stories for students to reference on my website, combatstinkythinking.com. (My call sign in the Air Force was "Stinky," so I had to have some fun with it.)

The Greek myth of Icarus, which many of us are familiar from childhood storybooks, was a kind of fatherly backdrop for me as I wrote this book, given the parallel to my own life. Icarus's story captures a father's instincts regarding awareness of our children's ambitions as they launch into the world—an awareness that is closely connected to our love and concern for their welfare.

Many young adults are like I was at that time, uncertain about launching away from Mom and Dad's house. The content in this book is intended to help. It may be that you're the parent, teacher, professor, coach, mentor, peer, colleague, or guidance counselor of a student you're helping launch. Being involved in our own brood's launch showed us the overwhelming amount of information now available for them to filter. So much information and so many distractions, but too little mentoring, guidance counselor resources, after-school sports participation, and family and social gatherings available to help guide them: that's the challenge for all students today.

Additionally, affordability exerts a perceptible "haves and have-nots" effect on school choices, youth sports participation, parental participation, after-school organizational programs, and college admissions here in the United States. One less-noticeable effect is on a third-party resource important for students in search of identity outside their family bubble. As of May 2019, the national student-to–guidance counselor ratio is 455:1. That is a lot of students for one counselor to listen to, empathize with, seek to understand, and guide, given the level of distraction and "stinkythinking" permeating adolescence. The American School Counselor Association (ASCA) recommends a ratio of 250:1.

Given this backstory, then, "Who is this father writing about *InCentivE$* for CREATEing our way, and what makes him credible or worth listening to?" My goal here is to inspire young adults and those who mentor them through shared stories demonstrating vulnerability and credibility. Let me introduce myself. I'm 54 years old, so the young adult years have left the station for me. My oldest child is 22. She's in the preliminary stages of launching into her young adult years, and we have three more kids behind her. I grew up in Miami, Florida, in the 1970s and early 80s. Great rock 'n' roll and reggae, fake IDs, beer, the beach, swimming, divorced parents, an awesome little brother, a lawn business, my own VW Bug purchase, *Miami Vice*, and a decent amount of partying, mischief and bad behavior. If not for the words of my high school guidance counselor, an Air Force Admissions Liaison Officer, and some nurturing words from older, wiser family members, Darwin's "survival of the fittest" rule would have worked against me long ago. Fortunately, these folks managed to inspire me to create my way, despite my guidance counselor's doubts and community college recommendations. This book is about inspiration and developing a strong character, making us capable of creating our own path, regardless of obstacles, pundits, experts, advice, brainwashing, indoctrination, propaganda, and social agenda. I want to provide a framework for young adults, their parents, teachers, coaches, mentors, and peers to use interactively as a continuous guidance package designed for developing characteristics that can help young adults create their *own* way, despite adversity, privilege, or entitlement.

I've experienced good and bad, shame and pride, loss and gain, failure and success in my fifty-four years. Nothing about my journey so far has been certain. Our growing-up stories are probably not very different: divorce; absent parents, loving parents; good neighborhoods, bad neighborhoods; good school, bad school; rich, poor; smothered, spoiled; single moms, single dads; abandonment; drug use, alcohol; truancy. These circumstances can describe any number of childhoods. The key word there is *childhood*. But now you're entering *adulthood*, so let's regard the childhood stuff as lessons learned, experiences noted. And then let's get on with life and its uncertainties.

Our mission on these pages is to inspire you. But wait—who's included in that "our"? You don't think I know how to write a book all by myself, do you? A lot of people are going to help me get this book to you, which makes this a team effort. I may want to inspire young adults, to motivate, guide, and teach, but I need a lot of people to help me reach those goals and distribute this book.

So in what way do we want to inspire you? We want to inspire you to figure out *who* you are so that you can match it up with *what* it is you want to create for your life. Sounds simple, right? Well, not exactly. It takes work. Like solving a math problem, it's a process. (My kids roll their eyes when I say this.) There is no pride of ownership in the process I'm about to share with you. This is simply something I've thought a lot about after spending time as an Air Force Admissions Liaison Officer, visiting high schools and seeing the same lost, confused, anxious, excited, angry, happy, sad, misinformed, misguided youths similar to what I was like over thirty years earlier. I started thinking, "I wonder if I could reach back to this period in my life, apply what I've learned from my own mistakes over the years and formulate a checklist process for young adults to reference, something to help them plan out their game beyond the post–high school launch." And here we are now, over thirty years since my high school graduation, and I'm finally able to chat with you about it. Life gets busy when you finish up those young adult years, trust me.

We all make mistakes in life. I certainly have. Guidance counselors, extended family, and great mentors influenced my life positively. I worry that we may be losing the connections to these resources that are so valuable for developing ourselves as future leaders and educators today, as we're distracted by a nonstop stream of social media, instant-gratification entertainment, video games, celebrity bad behavior, poor government, political, and C-suite leadership examples, news networks telling us how to think, and government-mandated educational curricula impairing teachers' abilities to influence and inspire young adults. Granted, not all of the people in these areas are bad actors, but we don't hear so much about the good ones unless we search for them on TED Talks or other less ratings-oriented and more positive forums.

I may not have specific, targeted answers to the complexity of these issues. But I can be intentional and focused in writing to students, parents, and guardians about seeking out mentoring resources, sharing the lessons I've learned, and providing a checklist with character development tools to consider. We might even be able to put a dent in reducing our 455:1 national student-to–guidance counselor ratio on our own, if this book resonates and adds value to others' lives.

I believe our current cultural perception of *InCentivE$* is framed around thinking in terms of wealth and power. One of my objectives in this book is to reframe our thinking about *InCentivE$* to be in terms of becoming healthy and empowered. In a way, I'm advocating for putting the spiritual before the material. I refer to spiritual development in a character formation way, not in a religious way. My vision is for students to be equipped with the tools for CREATEing their way—the tools I wish I had known when I was a young adult. I want students and their peers influencing an *ICE* age prioritizing *Integrity*, *Commitment*, and setting positive *Examples* for others. I want them to seek out mentoring and guidance counseling in face-to-face relationships from people who have "been there and done" what they may be interested in exploring, instead of just searching for disconnected information online.

There is no pride of authorship for the process I'll share with you in this book. Other experienced parents and professionals are encouraged to comment upon these thoughts for consideration within my blog. I designed the process for easy reference as a guide to matching our *who* to a *what*. The process is iterative, and ongoing accounting for flexibility in our *what* changes over time. Our young adult *what* doesn't necessarily mean graduating high school and going on to college. In fact, there has never been a better time in history to earn a living doing what you enjoy. I bet that *InCentivE$* for CREATEing our way will be a healthy tool for empowering young adults. Moving the needle from our normalized cultural definition of success—"wealth and power"—will not be an easy task. I don't minimize the importance of self-reliance and earning a living within our cultural norms. Rather, I'm encouraging a process for discovering self-reliance by earning a living in alignment with and in consideration of what young adults value individually, so they can find their personal flow states. Character matters on this journey. These young adult years are foundational. My kids are still learning and exploring the virtues, habits, and principled guidance written here.

My wish is for the thoughts shared in this book to influence my children and other readers to create their own way throughout the various stages of their lives, equipped with strong character, able to course-correct when finding themselves "flying too close to the sun"!

PART 2:

Lessons Learned

CHAPTER 1 | THE CREATE CHECKLIST:

C is for Clarity

Clarity of purpose is not something most of us acquire in high school. That's normal. There's nothing wrong with not having any idea what we want to do after high school graduation. This is no indication that we're behind our peers or exhibiting "loser" characteristics. Traditionally, we've filled this "clarity gap" with the culturally accepted norm of going to college. But what if we were to learn a way to develop clarity before finishing high school? What if we had a checklist we could follow and a process we could take with us to class during our daily activities that would help us discover clarity? This is the question that the CREATE checklist answers. CREATE stands for *Clarity, Relationships, Emotional intelligence, Add value, Tenacity,* and *Enthusiasm.*

The first letter, C, is for *clarity.* You've heard people talk about "finding clarity," but what we haven't discussed as much is a process for discovering clarity. Does clarity just happen one day, or is there something we can do, a tool we can use, to develop it? If clarity is the target, then how can we tactically solve the problem of hitting it? The OODA loop is the tactic I've chosen. OODA stands for *Observe, Orient, Decide,* and *Act.* The loop is a tool created by John Boyd. We'll learn how to take this loop with us to class and apply it to our everyday lives.

John Boyd was an American fighter pilot who commanded a group of pilots flying the F-86 in the Korean War. At the time, the F-86 was generally inferior to the MiG-15. However, "40-second Boyd" (he told his pilots he could be at their six o'clock in 40 seconds or less) encouraged his pilots not to focus on the MiG's superiority but on the mind of its operator. He advocated that they first observe the enemy pilot's initial move; second, orienting their aircraft in an advantageous three-dimensional position in relation to the bandit, decide on a course of action, delaying the MiG's initial turn advantage; then act upon that decision and fatigue the MiG pilot. See, though it's inferior to the MiG-15's maneuverability, the F-86 had fully hydraulic flight controls. The MiG-15 had hydraulically *assisted* flight controls, which require a lot more manhandling from the pilot. The American pilots could easily fly the F-86 without fatigue, whereas the MiG-15 pilot soon struggled to muscle the controls during a dogfight. If Boyd could get his pilots to think clearly and manage the fight by observing the initial move, orienting their lift vector advantageously to prolong the battle, deciding on an advantageous three-dimensional position, and acting on this decision, then they could get their minds off the MiG's advantages and focus instead on the man inside the machine—a pilot growing increasingly fatigued by the machine's disadvantages. It worked. The pilots would wear down the Korean pilots into making mistakes generated by Boyd's OODA loop during the dogfight. The end result? A lot more MiG fighter pilots in parachutes.

"But what does this have to do with young adults, strong character, and creating my pathway? I'm not fighting an enemy opponent." The opponent during adolescence is usually in our own minds, and we're going to learn to outmaneuver it.

> "*Know thy enemy as we know ourselves.*"
> – SUN TZU
>
> "*We have met the enemy and they are ours.*"
> – COMMODORE OLIVER HAZARD PERRY, ON THE WAR OF 1812

To paraphrase Commodore Perry: I have met the enemy, and the enemy is me.

Young adults face a lot of distractions beyond just their smartphones. And they see a lot of post-high-school-oriented cliché advice and stinkythinking—it swirls around hallways and classrooms. "Go to college," "You can't do this," "You should do that," "That's not realistic," "There's no money in that," and one of my favorites, "How do you expect to earn a living doing that?" A lot of us grow up programmed and conditioned by the expectations of others, never taking the opportunity to stop, think, regroup, and learn what it is that makes us tick individually. Soon we're out of the young adult years and raising a family, with responsibilities and ruts on a road we never imagined we'd end up driving. There is beauty in this scenario if we are prepared to adjust to obstacles along the way. Sometimes, however, our story takes us through years of trial, error, and growth to overcome what may in hindsight be considered the result of misapplied young adult years. But if we're deliberate about our path, follow a checklist, and learn to use the OODA loop for clarity, this won't happen. No matter what stage of life we're in, there's always a road to a more joyful present moment. We have to choose it—but choice is developed through education, experience, guidance, and guts.

The OODA loop equips us with a process for making choices and taking action, putting us on a path toward clarity. We're going to take the loop with us to class and learn how to apply it in our daily lives, building the habit of making choices and taking action. I add a B to the OODA loop to bring Boyd's work into the twenty-first century with its high-speed, max-information, and distraction character. The B stands for *Be present*. The 24/7, attached-at-the-hip social media devices we carry around make it difficult to consciously apply the loop if we aren't sufficiently in the moment to complete the loop. We can call this the BOODA loop. We need to *Be present* when we show up to learn something new, listening to our teachers, coaches, or mentors, as we apply the Observe, Orient, Decide, and Act process. Checking our phones for a Snapchat or being distracted by the pings and vibrations of our smartphones takes us out of being mindful of the moment we're currently experiencing, interrupting our ability to complete the clarity loop. Manage the smartphone distractions by turning it off or stuffing it in your backpack so that you can be mindfully present and focused on the moment to exercise the loop. You can reference my CREATE blog at combatstinkythinking.com for a brief explanation of the checklist, or whenever you think, "What did that stand for again?" I provide an example of using the loop in history class, and a YouTube link further explaining the process. For now, let's dive deeper into the loop and build our processing skills for finding clarity.

CHAPTER 2 | THE BOODA LOOP

Do stuff. Be clenched, curious. Not waiting for inspiration's shove or society's kiss on your forehead. Pay attention. It's all about paying attention. Attention is vitality. It connects you with others. It makes you eager. Stay eager. – Susan Sontag

I think that my job is to observe people and the world, and not judge them. I always hope to position myself away from so-called conclusions. I would like to leave everything wide open to all the possibilities in the world. – Haruki Murakami

Be Present

Ok, so as discussed at the end of our Clarity chapter, I added a B to John's loop, asking that we become mindful of *Being present*, and undistracted when exercising his loop. We've often heard our teachers tell us to focus on the task at hand. We want to do our best to eliminate distractions in our learning environments and get the most out of discovering clarity while executing the loop. Again, I'm recommending this additional preparatory step in Boyd's loop after years of observing my own children and their peers struggle to manage their attention between the conflicting interests of rapidly advancing information technology, gaming at their fingertips, social media connection, and classroom instruction. Therefore, it's important to reiterate our conscious decision to Be present before taking on Boyd's first step in the OODA loop. This sets us up for "paying attention," as Susan Sontag recommends in her quote above.

Next up is to Observe.

Observe

"Observe what?" Today we're going to observe our "who," not our "what." We want to gather data about ourselves from multiple sources. These data include our personal circumstances and situations. Who am I? What has influenced me? What do I enjoy doing? How do I know I enjoy doing something? Easy: when we lose track of time while doing something, we are probably enjoying this activity. We are "in the zone," as they say, or in a state of flow. Where do my parents, coaches, teachers, mentors, peers, and extended family members see my personality, talents, and interests aligning? These questions are "observation." None of these observations is to be taken personally in a critical way but only in an overall, constructive way to gain an idea of how we are perceived. We're interested in where others see our talents taking us, and we wonder if there is anything we may have missed or have been unaware of that now seems like, "Wow! I didn't notice this about myself." As we go through this looping process, you'll probably end up back at the top, over and over again, mindful of lessons learned observing and reassessing after the initial *Action* step. It's after this first succession of the loop that we may discover, "I'm not so good with blood and guts on operating tables." The lather–rinse–repeat BOODA process cycles back, restarting the process with lessons learned. The idea of continuing the loop is to end up aligning the *who* we are with the *what* it is we want to create for ourselves. At age 54, I'm still looping. It's a fun process of constant refining and reinvention—a continuum. Writing is my new one, and someday it may become my old one.

That's what the CREATE guidance process is all about: constant iteration and reinvention. Figure 3 is an illustrative example of our BOODA loop:

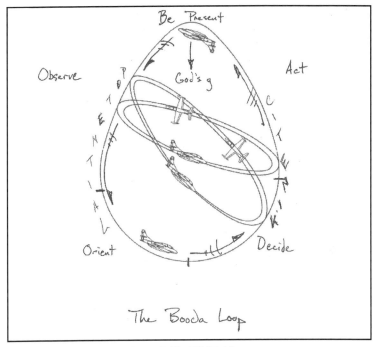

Figure 2. The BOODA loop.

The BOODA loop shown is a rudimentary overlay from an old Navy description of the fighter pilot energy egg that I've modified for illustrative purposes. We begin the loop at the top by *Being present*. The top of the egg represents our greatest God-given potential, equivalent to the extra 1g force of gravity that fighter pilots think about when engaging an enemy in a three-dimensional aerial fight. God's g is the supreme intelligence's potential energy contribution to improving our fighter aircraft's turn performance when our aircraft's lift vector from the wings is pointed toward Mother Earth. When we consciously include God's g potential in our game plan, we are maximizing our potential energy and minimizing our kinetic energy required for the quickest tightest turns for defeating our enemy. This is why the illustration is shaped like an egg. A fighter aircraft's turn radius is tighter at the top of the loop given the same turning g held due to God's additional

1g of performance. In essence, we get 3 g's of turn radius performance at a cost of only 2 g's of energy. Holding the same g throughout our loop scribes a tighter turn in the top half of the energy egg because of God's g. Today, for our discussion, God's g represents our innate talents, interests, skill sets, joy, and ambition. We intend to work with our God-given potential as we align our who with a what. Observation of our who begins by identifying the things we enjoy doing; what others see as our talents, propensities, or limitations; and what our older, more experienced mentors believe fits our personality and style. Who we are is inclusive of physical, mental, and moral aspects of our environment. Think in broad terms in the observation phase of the loop. When we've collected these data, we start to orient ourselves in relation to these observations. A simple observational example may be recognizing our interest in how buildings are constructed. The next step could be to orient ourselves toward math, geometry, tools, machines, carpentry, or architecture. We might then decide to find classes in carpentry, architecture, shop, design, or heavy equipment operation. We act by participating in the classes we select, reassessing our interest along the way. When finished with class, we start the loop all over again, incorporating any new observations for adjusting our course toward certain aspects of construction we found most interesting. We could pivot altogether and find joy only in the operation of the heavy equipment. Each trip through the loop, each revolution, funnels us closer and closer to our "clarity" target.

Take me, for example. My life-changing moment was when my father had pretty much had enough of my stuff and told me, "Kid, you're on your own when you turn 18." I was a senior in high school at the time and uncertain what I wanted to do with myself post-graduation. What I knew was I no longer wanted to be a doctor but that I was supposed to go to college. There was a day, however, in the spring of my junior year, while babysitting my cousin, that I saw an inspiring TV commercial of an F-14 Tomcat landing on an aircraft carrier deck in the middle of a pristine blue ocean. After the fighter successfully trapped the wire on deck and came to a stop, a big yellow "Fly Navy" banner appeared on the screen. I was smitten. I guess this was the beginning of my personal *Observation* phase. I'd been exposed to flying through my father and thought it was cool and probably a fun thing to do. I enjoyed watching war films, with fighter aircraft protecting bombers and dogfighting the Germans. I enjoyed racing sailboats and spearfishing in the ocean. I often thought it would be neat to sail around the world. And there it was on TV: flying, boating, and world travel, in one commercial. I made this *Observation* in the spring of my junior year and began *Orienting* my priorities around this observation in the fall, after my father made it clear that I was on my own. I *Decided* to start asking a lot of people, mentors, and guidance counselors how I could end up flying fighters off aircraft carriers. I learned and *Acted* by applying to the U.S. Naval Academy. Six months later, the continuous and unconscious application of the OODA looping process brought me to receiving a letter offering me an appointment to the U.S. Air Force Academy Preparatory School. We weren't plugged into the smartphone matrix back in those days, so *Being present* and undistracted in the moment we were experiencing was more the norm. Receiving that appointment was my lucky break in life. I was fortunate to have positioned myself with the help of family, mentors, coaches and friends.

Here are some sample observation questions to ask:

1. What activities do I most enjoy doing?
2. Am I adventurous and outgoing, or do I prefer peace and quiet?
3. Am I social—not in a media sense, but in a meeting-and-talking-with-people sense?
4. Do I know what I want to do to earn a living?
5. Am I more interested in having a lot of money or in doing something I enjoy to earn a living?
6. Would I enjoy joining the military and serving my country?
7. Do my coaches believe my sports performance is or can be Division 1 material for scholarships and a possible professional future?

8. Is there an area of study I found most interesting in school and would like to pursue further?

9. Do my parents, teachers, and friends feel I'm creative and artistic?

10. Do I like to design and build?

11. What makes me feel purposeful or fulfilled when I'm doing it?

12. How do I feel when I help others?

13. Do I believe the "sky is the limit" for me? If not, why?

14. Besides my parents, who would be a reputable resource for me to talk to about my future?

15. Whom do my parents recommend as a reputable resource to discuss my future?

16. Of all of my family members, colleagues, peers, coaches, teachers, mentors...who stands out as my most admired, and why? (Eliminate concerns about offending anyone with this answer.)

Do we really know ourselves as young adults? Do our schools teach us to learn who we are as individuals, or is it only about reading, writing, and arithmetic? According to a *Miami Herald* article from 2007, traditionally our school guidance counselors were outnumbered 287 students to 1. Today, according to the American School Counselor Association (ASCA), our national student to counselor ratio is closer to 455:1. This ratio doesn't favor the likelihood of receiving one-on-one guidance and wisdom from someone other than the parents we tend to rebel against as young adults. I find this statistic motivational for proactively seeking out mentoring resources on our own.

Be mindful of Haruki Murakami's suggestion above to observe people and the world, remaining non-judgmental, avoiding conclusions and remaining wide open to all possibilities. Now that we have a pretty good feel for the *Observe* part of the loop, let's spend some time on *Orient*.

Orient

We suggest that you consistently work throughout your lifetime on the creation of a coherent and integral spirit body. If your mind never turns to the spiritual in life, why do you think it will turn to the spirit in death? If you are not "at home" with the things spiritual, why do you think you will be able to orient yourself when you are thrust into the spirit world? At best, you will become disoriented and uncomfortable. – Laurence Galian

If I continually focus on what I don't have, my life will always be completely empty despite the fact that it's completely full. – Craig D. Lounsbrough

Orientation is the most important position in the loop. This is where we do the analysis of our *who* in relation to our *what*. This is where we start crunching the data we gathered from *Observation* and analyze them in relation to our genetics, cultural background, previous experiences, interests, and so forth. Here we look for any mismatches, errors in judgment, or standout information we may have missed about ourselves that we can now use to our advantage in pursuit of our what. This is the moment in the loop when Boyd recommended that his fighter pilots orient their aircraft lift vector to demand the MiG's pilot to turn more often during the fight. More turns created cumulative pilot fatigue errors, eliminating the MiG's turn performance advantage (less g–capable pilot = wider, less loaded turns). The F-86's hydraulic flight controls soon allowed our pilots to perform to the maximum in their jets throughout the engagement, and then saddle up and shoot down the tired pilot inside the MiG.

Let's play out the significance of an "orient" scenario that we can all relate to today. Let's pretend we are Lin Manuel Miranda, on our way to history class armed with BOODA loop awareness. "History, boooring!" we might say. Today's class lesson is the story of the contribution of one of America's founding fathers to the development of our republic of representative democracy.

Miranda mindfully and respectfully gives his attention to his teacher, who put in the time to develop and present the lesson. Upon observing the lesson, Miranda begins orienting his love for musical performance in relation to Alexander Hamilton's incredible story. He decides to explore connecting hip-hop and rap lyrics and music to Hamilton's storyline, and then he takes action by gathering resources and developing songs and scenes for actors to play out. He includes his talented and creative colleagues and puts together a team to create the Broadway musical masterpiece we all know today, *Hamilton*. It's a perfect example of orienting one's God-given talents and family influences toward creating a beautiful *what*.

I included the quotes by Galian and Lounsbrough at the beginning of this section to emphasize a continuous growth-oriented mindset. We'll get to specific character-building tools for developing this mindset while discussing the *E* step of our checklist, where we apply the *InCentivE$* acronym to develop our emotional intelligence. Galian's quote advocates that we never stop learning and grounding ourselves during our limited time in this universe. He wants us to be curious, to think, and to be oriented and comfortable when our time is up. Lounsbrough's quote suggests that we make the most of what we've got. Adolescence is the time we might be besieged by negative, comparative thinking. This kind of stinkythinking keeps us in a low-energy, non-growth-oriented state of mind, fighting against God's g versus working with it. When we think of our lives as "full," we appreciate our universal uniqueness while engaging in the BOODA loop. The orient phase is about aligning our interests around our observations in relation to the data and experiences presented thus far.

I've mentioned Lounsbrough's quote after interacting with many students who demonstrated an affinity for negative, culturally normative stinkythinking. "My grades suck." "My SAT scores are terrible." "No college is going to accept me." "I'm not good with my hands." "My parents can't afford college." "I'm not good with authority." I've heard quite a few self-defeating attitudes over the years, many of which we can attribute to the assumption that wealth and power are not accessible to the people suffering assumed negative circumstances. This is silly stinkythinking conditioning brought on by entertainment, advertising, marketing, sales, social media, and political agendas.

It's simply too early in our lives to believe any limiting thoughts or buy into any propaganda streaming through our phones. Our lives are full, as Lounsbrough states. Our goal is to orient our fullness toward a meaningful course. Once we've oriented ourselves around the initial observation of marrying music to the story of Alexander Hamilton, or setting the stage for becoming a fighter pilot, then it's time to make some decisions about how to get there.

Decide

You have brains in your head. You have feet in your shoes. You can steer yourself in any direction you choose. You're on your own, and you know what you know. And you are the guy who'll decide where to go. – Dr. Seuss

The most difficult thing is the decision to act, the rest is merely tenacity. The fears are paper tigers. You can do anything you decide to do. You can act to change and control your life; and the procedure, the process is its own reward. – Amelia Earhart

We're over the top orientating ourselves so as to take advantage of God's g, using our potential energy to transition into the full g-strain inner afterburner kinetic phase of our loop. It's decision time. We've made some observations about ourselves. We've crunched the observational data and oriented ourselves advantageously toward our interest. Now we start deciding on our course of action. This is where many of us get stuck. We fear committing to any one decision, failing to act, comparing our interests to our peers, loitering around in a low-energy state, paralyzed while we analyze. Dr. Seuss nailed it in his quote above.

The most common decision-making problems young adults experience are characterized by feelings of doubt, uncertainty, or imperfection. We will be perplexed, confused, unsure, disoriented, bewildered, and unclear at times while creating our way. The *InCentivE$* character-building tool discussed in the emotional intelligence step of our checklist will help us deal with some of the stinkythinking that can hang us up. Strengthening our character with some virtues to practice and habits to exercise will help mitigate our indecisiveness. Remember, our objective is to create *our* way. We want to approach the decision phase of our loop emotionally intelligent, able to filter out everyone else's noise, improving our ability to decide in alignment with our interests versus all the pressures surrounding us. In a sense, we are becoming "situationally aware" as we enter this part of the loop. Working on our emotional intelligence helps us counter biases, clearing noisy obstructions from our path to decision. Here's a quick look at emotional intelligence, and then later we'll go into much more detail.

The best way I've found to summarize emotional intelligence is this description from mindtools.com:

Emotional intelligence (EI) is the ability to recognize your emotions, understand what they're telling you, and realize how your emotions affect people around you. It also involves your perception of others: when you understand how they feel, this allows you to manage relationships more effectively.

Relationships? Why do I care about relationships when creating my way? We are an interdependent, entangled society of humans. Involving other humans in our development helps us create our way; it's likely that the "been there, done that" experiences of other people will be relevant to our own personal circumstances. Anyone who believes that they got to their contented, creative place in life by themselves is not emotionally intelligent. We develop a plethora of relationships outside of Mom and Dad's guidance, and we want to effectively manage those relationships to find and create our way. These relationships give us frames of reference for making emotionally intelligent decisions.

So, we've observed, oriented—and now we need to decide. Let's say we think becoming a firefighter is the "what" that matches our "who." Great! Let's decide on a course of action. Leonardo Da Vinci teaches us an excellent mind-mapping technique. You can find details about it with an internet search for "Da Vinci mind map." We can create a mind map with this technique during the orient phase, specific to becoming a firefighter. Some possible ideas: visit my local fire station; ask for a ride-along; study fire sources; look for high school fire programs; attend Emergency Medical Technician training; become a lifeguard; take CPR; find a local firefighter to be a mentor; visit websites; read books. When we've written these ideas on a sheet of paper, we build a map that goes from the easy things we can do right now, down to the more difficult things we'll need to accomplish while navigating to our target. We decide on courses of action. What do I need to do right now to achieve my ultimate goal of becoming a firefighter? Start there and get moving. Remember what Amelia Earhart said: "The most difficult thing is the decision to act."

Figure 4 is a sample mind map for becoming a fighter pilot:

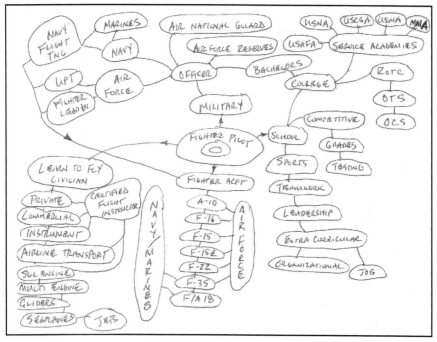

Figure 3. Fighter pilot mind map.

Deciding to go a particular direction doesn't hinder our ability to change direction somewhere down the road. Many of us wonder whether we are making the right decision—but make a decision anyway and see where it takes you. We can always course-correct. Life is uncertain and this will never change. We'll always have doubts and uncertainty, throughout every stage of our lives. But we need to get in the arena and participate anyway. Decide to move in a direction, test your theories, pass, fail, or succeed after following through with your action, modifying your course based on the results of your action. This is a *life* cycle, not just a *launch* cycle. Many of us feel imperfect or not good enough to pursue a course of action. Nonsense! How do you know if you don't try? How many people have we encountered who say, "If I could do it, anyone can do it"? They jumped in, got knocked down a few times, and got back up, better equipped to finish or change course. Once we decide on a course to pursue, it's time to act.

Act

Thinking is easy, acting is difficult, and to put one's thoughts into action is the most difficult thing in the world. – Johann Wolfgang von Goethe

This is as true in everyday life as it is in battle: we are given one life and the decision is ours whether to wait for circumstances to make up our mind, or whether to act, and in acting, to live. – Omar N. Bradley

I agree with Goethe about some of the reasons we get hung up during the decision-making part of our loop. We suffer analysis paralysis. We rationalize indecision. We weigh costs versus benefits in time and money. This delays our action. In addition, we've become so conditioned to a need for instant gratification that any process which seems lengthy in terms of results challenges our patience. Our conditioning makes it difficult for us to see actions through to a logical conclusion of pass, fail, or revamp. We'll address this challenge later with our *InCentivE$* discussion to help equip students with the right tools.

Regardless, once we decide on a course of action for becoming a fire-fighter, we need to act on this decision. In my opinion, this is the easiest part of our BOODA loop. Most of our mental energy went into observation, orientation, and deciding. Now we translate this investment of potential energy into kinetic energy by executing. We go to college. We take the classes. We visit the firehouse. We become an Emergency Medical Technician. We get flying lessons. We take acting, singing, and improv lessons. Whatever we do, at the completion of each action, we observe, orient, decide, and act all over again to keep on our course or to reassess or change our course. A fire department ride-along to see a few motorcycle or car accidents may be enough for us to know whether to continue our current pursuit or alter our course.

Boyd wanted his pilots to observe the man in the MiG cockpit and orient their aircrafts' initial moves to delay the MiG's superior maneuverability from achieving weapons employment parameters. Delaying or extending the fight long enough by employing energy management and proper lift vector control in relation to the bandit's maneuvers would fatigue the MiG pilot as he works the flight controls under g-induced stress. By wearing him down physically, our pilots used the OODA loop to capitalize on the bandit's fatigue-induced fighter maneuver errors. The longer the fight, the more fatigued the MiG pilots became, which allowed our pilots to manipulate the hydraulic flight controls of their F-86 into a superior position from which to fire upon the tired, turning enemy. I know what some of you are thinking: "How could our pilots delay against another aircraft's superior turning advantage?" The energy egg, God's g, and another entire book on basic fighter maneuvers (BFM) are all good places to start. But essentially, during the Korean air conflict Boyd taught his men to orient their aircraft in relation to the man flying the machine rather than to the machine itself. He trained them to *decide* on a pursuit course requiring the MiG to turn more, and then *acting* so as to manage this pursuit course to take advantage of God's g and capitalize on fighter errors until bingo: bullets, missiles, fuel, or a pilot floating down in a parachute.

The BOODA loop is simply a tool for paying attention and helping us discover our personal interests instead of just the ones we take from others or from TV or smartphones. The process requires us to follow through and follow up, always intent upon shedding light on whether our interest remains fantasy or becomes reality. The action step clarifies our interest's transition from fantasy to reality. The action step feeds us back into the loop, with either "I like where this is going" or "maybe not," setting us up for our next iteration. Each progression of the loop gains ground on our *Clarity* target.

Remember the recommendation from famous WWII commander General Omar Bradley: "we are given one life and the decision is ours whether to wait for circumstances to make up our mind, or whether to act, and in acting, to live." Now that we have an idea how to use the BOODA loop to develop and discover clarity, it's time to move on to the next step of our CREATE checklist: *R is for Relationships.*

CHAPTER 3:

R is for Relationships

If you want to go fast, go alone. If you want to go far, go together. – Proverb

Negativity has the power to destroy everything. Don't let it. – Sarah Freedom, from www.sarahfreedom.com (Pinterest quotes)

Every new virtual connection is making you less human. – Sarah Freedom, from www.sarahfreedom.com (Pinterest quotes)

We can't get where we want to go without help from others. Be grateful for parents, teachers, mentors, peers, colleagues, guidance counselors, and the extended network of family, friends, and the universally connected entanglement of humans along our journey, helping us create our way. I included the above quotes for you to consider because they're relevant today and speak about the consequences of deceasing human relationships. I advocate that we adults help turn this trend around for our young adults by sponsoring events, developing more opportunities for our children to connect, and building relationships with others. With so many activities coming under assault from affordability, requiring both parents to work, there are far fewer nondigital human connections happening today. Observing mannerisms, behaviors, nonverbal communication, and emotional connection teaches us perspective and context in the sharing of interests and information.

Most of us want an identity outside our parental bubble. We're different apples, despite coming from similar trees. Our educational system recognized this a long time ago and created guidance counselor positions within the school systems to give students access to a third-party sounding board. Guidance counselors do their jobs amazingly well, but their numbers are dwindling in relation to the number of students they're being asked to counsel. The numbers preclude realistic expectations that this third-party resource is being given adequate opportunity to benefit students today. Many school guidance counselors are recent college graduates with few life experiences of their own to share as they connect and identify with students. Students and guidance counselors need our help.

We're not interacting face-to-face or socializing in person nearly as much as in the past. This is reducing our exposure to mentoring opportunities from people we meet around the dinner table or in casual conversation during parties. Guidance and mentoring are difficult to project from a smartphone or a Zoom call. Human interaction, connection, and animated speaking with nonverbal cues make conversation clearer and more meaningful. There's less room for misinterpretation and misperception. We need to see students' faces light up or sulk down when sharing with them our "been there, done that" stories. Today we arguably spend less time around dinner tables, campfires, or family get-togethers, and more time alone on our phones. This is not an efficient or effective method for building relationships that help us discover our who and create our what.

The proverb at the beginning of this section reminds us, "If you want to go fast, go alone. If you want to go far, go together." Our attention spans have shortened tremendously with the advent of smartphones and the instantly gratifying 24/7 social feed at our fingertips. Every lull in conversation can now be filled by glancing at our phones. Teaching my kids how to safely fix a flat tire or change the oil in the car was almost an act of futility. "Why, Dad? Just pay someone to fix it. <ding> [sound of Snapchat alert]." Asking them to put their phones away for a minute didn't solve the problem, because the fear of missing out (FOMO) on something from their phone still robbed me of their attention. Learning how to do anything laborious, as my father and mother taught me, could not compete with the new paradigm of the four-inch screen. The best my wife and I could do now is to learn to manage this new normal by setting a good example and capitalizing on the moments when we had the kids' attention. Getting angry or dealing out punishment seemed unproductive and ineffective, given that the current situation had become this generation's normal. We had to manage it, not punish it. "Going fast" in the proverb advocates for our patience and inclusion of others to enhance our journey. Entrepreneurs who don't credit their business success to surrounding themselves with people who share in the growth of the business are the exception. You need a team. There will be good, bad, and ugly players on the team, but every relational experience on your team drives forward momentum. It's a lot easier not to involve anyone else, not to become bogged down by someone else's advice for speed—but eventually you will reach the limit of your experience and knowledge, where the inclusion of others would have carried you places you never thought possible. Going fast works for some things, like running a foot race, but not when trying to figure out who you are, where your talents lie, and what may be a logical next step in creating our way. We have to take the time to involve others and their experiences in determining a post–high school game plan that's in alignment with our personality and interests. Going alone is slower than going together when it comes to our young, inexperienced adult decision-making. If you want to create your way more quickly, don't be afraid to sit down and open up with your guidance counselor, coach, extended family members, or a vetted and trusted mentor. Intentionally seek out positive people to balance any negative thinking that sometimes seems to come more naturally. Speaking of negativity, let's spend some time discussing it.

"Negativity has the power to destroy everything." Cynics, critics, sass, smartass, profane lyrics, road rage, disrespectful social media, fake news, and poor celebrity examples of humanity are the negativity many of us have transferred our allegiance to. These sources think for us, entertain us, and encourage our cynicism in return for likes, ratings, and profits. We're becoming less and less familiar with our constitutional protections, leaving us vulnerable to subtle removal of the freedom it was designed to protect. Our rights and privacy seem to be constantly under attack. The fact is, negativity sells.

But does it sell well enough to have the power to destroy everything, as the quote suggests? Defunding the police, whose duty is to preserve law and order and ensure public safety seems to be a negative overreaction to something that leadership, education, training, and accountability could reasonably address, without fearing that our 9-1-1 calls will go unanswered. We can exercise civil protesting without looting, injury, and death. We can make citizenship, pathways, and benefits in legal immigration topics worthy of positive discussion in our educational institutions. We can positively discuss the benefits of freedom of speech, supported through journalistic integrity, weighed against agendas, profiteering, and entertainment.

I think that a lot of the negativity surrounding the issue examples above is occurring because, as the quote suggests, we are becoming less human in our interaction and relationships. We'll rant on Twitter, but without seeking to understand the context of another. We are bold digitally, and weak socially. We are arrogant typists and cowardly conversationalists. It does seem that social negatives outweigh our positives when we tune into media and entertainment, which leads us to our next concern: that virtual connections make us less human.

Without context, it's difficult to know when we are being presented only one side of a virtual story. We aren't able to distinguish truth from lies when we can't see the nonverbal cues, emotional reactions, or environmental distractions. It's a challenge to interpret delayed, grainy, virtual responses, or to empathize with the unintended consequences of social justice discourse without emotionally intelligent leadership, reporting, media, and entertainment. If all we reference is the targeted messages on our TVs, phones, and computers, but without experiencing human relationships to counter or validate the claims, then we are ripe for conditioning to negativity.

We need to talk with one another, to agree to disagree and then seek to understand one another's perspectives, circumstances, and motivations. Relationships with our phones will not take us very far; relationships with people will. People will make us question our interests and challenge our thinking, connecting us with others who are like-minded or more knowledgeable. For forward momentum in our lives, nothing is more important or more effective than human connection. Relationships are vital for CREATEing our way. "Googling it" is not sufficient. Sitting down with another human and connecting over shared interests, even just slowly finding our way forward together, is the best way to go. Seeking mentors who have been there and done what we may be interested in experiencing is vital for our journey. We consider ourselves lucky when we find a mentor with a high emotional quotient (EQ). We'll be better at recognizing EQ characteristics after reading the next section. Emotional intelligence is the next step of our checklist.

CHAPTER 4:

E is for Emotional Intelligence (EI)

To enjoy good health, to bring true happiness to one's family, to bring peace to all, one must first discipline and control one's own mind. If a man can control his mind, he can find the way to Enlightenment, and all wisdom and virtue will naturally come to him. – Buddha

We are what we repeatedly do. Excellence, then, is not an act, but a habit. – Aristotle

Entire books have been written on the topic of emotional intelligence, also referred to as your "emotional quotient" (EQ). Here I'll simply repeat the definition we talked about earlier in our orient phase, and an acronym I've included for developing our EQ. Emotional intelligence is the capacity to be aware of, control, and express one's emotions, and to handle interpersonal relationships judiciously and empathetically.

Given the distractions of social media, never before has there been a time when emotional intelligence is so relevant for successfully navigating the creative process. Our intelligence quotient (IQ) is not as important as our EQ for creating and executing our post–high school game plan. Our "smart" factor is not as valuable as learning to become relatable in this stage of our lives. Most of us simply do not have the life experience, knowledge, or wisdom that we can substitute with our IQs. In a moment, we'll discuss *InCentivE$* for developing relatable characteristics and improving our EQ.

Remember in the introduction, when we talked about changing how we think about the word *InCentivE$*? We want to orient ourselves toward treating this word as a character-building tool rather than just "What's in it for me?" The material part ($) comes last, not first. We're going to break this word down into an acronym representing three key virtues and about seven habits. A virtue is a positive trait. We could come up with a huge number of positive traits to exemplify in one's character, but after a lot of thought and experience, failure and success, I've decided to focus on the three that I feel best complement our objective for creating our way: *Integrity, Commitment,* and setting a positive *Example.* The other letters of the word *InCentivE$* make up habits that I believe are important for manifesting a positive vector toward turning our dreams into realities. Remember, there is no pride in ownership here. As you become *ICE* men and *ICE* women, you can raise your own flags about the validity of these virtues and habits, and which you find more or less important in creating your way. These are a place to start, not to finish.

What is a habit? A habit is a behavior that's repeated regularly and tends to occur unconsciously. This is a big part of our lather–rinse–repeat BOODA loop process. Remember, we are young adults. We have formed some good habits and some bad ones in our childhood. What we want to do is capitalize on the good and minimize the bad. We want to be able to identify and minimize the limiting or self-defeating habits we've formed, whether by choice or by example, during our childhood. We aren't going to talk here about whether we have good habits or bad ones. Instead, we're going to discuss good ones we want to incorporate into our routine. Let's discuss the virtues and habits.

On the next page is the handout I wrote for my kids not long after my F-16 accident. After reading, we'll discuss the *InCentivE$* acronym for developing our emotional intelligence as we progress through the remainder of the CREATE checklist.

3 seconds to impact and 0.87 seconds to live...

YOUR DAD'S INCENTIVE$ FOR CREATING YOUR WAY

INTEGRITY

The Air Force Academy taught us to live honorably by not lying, cheating, or stealing, or tolerating that behavior from others. They taught us to be impeccable with our words, to fess up when we mess up, and not to gossip about others. Strive to live your lives this way.

"NO"

"No": learn to say this word in an empowering way. Establish your priorities, and don't compromise them when you feel pressure from your peers. Be aware of and prepared for the consequences when you do.

COMMITMENT

You can't know your true strengths, weaknesses, or abilities unless you "warrior up" and commit to getting in the arena. Fear is when your mind and body are in a heightened state of awareness. Courage to commit is fear's opponent. Participate, and you will learn to manage fear.

EGO

There are "Good, Bad, and Ugly" egos. Surround yourself with the good ones. Try not to take another's criticism of you personally, and don't compare yourself to them. Revel in and work with your universal uniqueness.

NAVIGATE

Learn to thoroughly read a map of terrain, obstacles and all. Find your position on the map, orient yourself, and move to a position of higher ground somewhere in the distance. Achieving your goals is the same process.

Remember, go from large to small identifying features that funnel you toward your target.

TRIPLE TIMES

Take time to train yourself physically; you'll feel better. Take time to think about the world critically and draw your own conclusions. Take time to thank and develop an attitude of gratitude.

INFORM

Maintain a desire to learn throughout your life. Actively listen to others and strive to understand before you talk.

VISUALIZE

Intention is picturing in your mind how the achievement of your goal tastes, smells, and feels. This intention will naturally bring you to the people, circumstances, and events necessary to realize your vision.

EXAMPLE

Whatever you are asked to do or choose to do for yourself in work, study, sport, or play is worth giving your best effort. Set a positive, inspiring example.

$EN¢E OF HUMOR

Find the humor in life's adversities. You'll make mistakes—get over it and forgive yourself. Experience the joy of being less serious, able to laugh at yourself along your way. Serving others will teach you humility. Remain humble and treat the dollar sign as the result of your journey, not its purpose.

Virtue 1:

I IS FOR INTEGRITY

The Air Force Academy taught us to live honorably by not lying, cheating, or stealing, or tolerating that behavior from others. They taught us to be impeccable with our words, to fess up when we mess up, and not to gossip about others. Strive to live your lives this way. – Peter Smith

The greatness of a man is not in how much wealth he acquires, but in his integrity and his ability to affect those around him positively. – Bob Marley

I was fortunate to survive my accident. Unfortunately, several things besides my wallet were in my flight suit pocket that evening—including a thumb drive where I'd been collecting ideas about a mentoring program for kids, with lessons I'd learned and intended to convey to my children when the timing was right. Obviously that thumb drive didn't make it during my night swim in the Gulf of Mexico. Also unfortunate was that my computer's hard drive had crashed several days before, losing all my work. The evening was shaping up to be an experience out of *A Series of Unfortunate Events*. One of the first things I did after the accident was put pen to paper, in case my ticket was prematurely punched successfully. "*InCentivE$* for CREATEing your way" was the something I put together. Very dramatic, I know, but I've enjoyed putting it together into this guidance package.

The first thing I want to talk to you about is integrity, and why this is so important in creating our way. I know it sounds pretty heavy when we think about "not lying, cheating, or stealing, nor tolerating that behavior from others," because as kids that's pretty much what we do, right? Few of us have not committed all of the above during our childhoods, let alone as adults. "No, Mom, I wasn't drinking beer with my buddies last night (wink, wink)." None of us has ever taken a peek at the smart guy's test paper in class, or tried to stuff a little crib sheet up our sleeve . . . right? Oh, and none of us has ever ended up with an extra candy bar in our pocket as we walk out of the grocery store. This is why we get "juvenile" status during our youth. Society says we ought to know better by the time we're eighteen, and now there will be consequences! We know kids are "all Mach and no vector" in their younger years as ego takes center stage. I heard a lot about this kind of behavior and how to avoid it in high school, but suddenly there were dire consequences for a young eighteen-year-old from Miami entering the U.S. Air Force Academy Preparatory School. Getting kicked out for violating the honor code was not going to happen to me, since I felt like I had already been given a huge break even receiving the opportunity. I wanted to fly fighter jets, and I was not about to jeopardize my shot. I learned to live with the honor code, but more importantly, I learned how liberating it is not to feel that I have to lie, cheat, or steal. I learned to be accountable, not make excuses, and to be responsible for my actions. It didn't take me long to see where the academy was going with this code. The United States invested taxpayer dollars in making me an officer for this country. The Treasury wants to ensure a return on their investment by developing national leaders of high moral character. They start with the honor code, and adherence to it has made me a much better person. Now, let me be clear: we're human, and there are nuances regarding integrity. If, for example, your wife asks you if she looks good in the plaid overalls with high heels, you might say yes when you really think no. This doesn't mean you lack integrity. This is called "tact," and it enters the "humane" category of interacting with others.

Speaking of interacting with others, there was a second part to my integrity quote above, about "our word, fessing up when we mess up and not gossiping about others." This was also a valuable lesson, discussed and rein- forced through ethics courses and self-study while I attended the academy. One of Miguel Ruiz's "Four Agreements" is to agree to be "impeccable with your word." All children are familiar with Mom or Dad saying, "If you don't have something nice to say about someone, don't say anything at all." Many of us fall short of this principle. When we develop the ability to be impeccable with our word, to fess up when we mess up and not gossip about others, we experience freedom and liberation from the burden of comparison. Do what we say and say what we do—"actions speak louder than words"—is an incredible place to find ourselves as a human being. The ability to not judge others or compare ourselves to others through gossip is liberating in accepting ourself and understanding that the "Universal Intelligence" does not intend for all of us to be the same. When we find ourselves appreciating others for their differences, or examining the circumstances behind the difference, we find ourself in a healthy place for *developing solutions* rather than *perpetuating problems*. Not a bad place to be, and a much happier feeling.

A quick glance at our news headlines about politics, business, sports, and even our military reminds us that we can always improve as Americans in integrity. The sooner we develop this virtue, the faster our progress will be toward the creation of our way, since we attract people into our lives who feel comfortable helping us succeed. Everyone wants to hang around a person who is accountable for their actions and speaks nicely about and plays well with others.

Safety investigation and accident boards are known for being uncomfortable situations in the Air Force. The board of inquiry pulls no punches in determining cause and assigning the dreaded "pilot error." Years of training, conditioning, and experience, and being surrounded by fellow officers with impeccable standards of integrity, made it easier for me to walk into the bright lights and microphones and admit that I had crashed a perfectly good airplane into the sea and wasn't sure how or why it happened—but that I was ready to figure it out so we could prevent it from happening to anyone else. Yes, I took question after question during the inquiry, but we drew many good lessons from my experience that will save another pilot someday. In fact, less than two years after my accident, our center pedestals were outfitted with improved avionics, instantly helping the pilot react swiftly to an unusual attitude. It's much easier to live as you learn to fess up when you mess up.

Defending yourself becomes hard if you lie, cheat, or steal, and tolerate that behavior from others. If we lack integrity, we waste a lot of defensive energy that could have been directed toward creating our way.

A good gauge of how we're doing with integrity is summed up in the old adage of "doing what's right when nobody is looking." Philosophers debate how an individual knows the difference between right and wrong. We know what it feels like to do right rather than wrong. Some circumstances are addressed in biblical parables regarding empathy toward the hungry whom we can feed, the cold whom we can offer a coat. Constitutionally, one of the greatest aspects of the United States is that we provide for people who are unable to help themselves.

What are some traits of living with integrity? I've paraphrased some great ones from *America's Air Force: A Profession of Arms:*

INTEGRITY FIRST

Integrity is simply doing the right thing, all the time, whether everyone is watching or no one is watching. It is the compass that keeps us on the right path when we are confronted with ethical challenges and personal temptations, and it is the foundation upon which trust is built. An individual realizes integrity when thoughts and actions align with what he or she knows to be right. The virtues that demonstrate one truly values integrity include:

HONESTY: Honesty is the hallmark of integrity. As public servants, we are trusted agents. Honesty requires us to evaluate our performance against standards, and to conscientiously and accurately report findings. It drives us to advance our skills and credentials through our own effort. The service member's word must be unquestionable. This is the only way to preserve the trust we hold so dear with each other and with the population we serve.

COURAGE: Courage is not the absence of fear, but doing the right thing despite the fear. Courage empowers us to take necessary personal or professional risks, make decisions that may be unpopular, and admit to our mistakes; having the courage to take these actions is crucial for the mission, the Air Force, and the nation.

ACCOUNTABILITY: Accountability is responsibility with an audience. That audience may be the American people, our units, our supervisors, our fellow airmen, our families, our loved ones, and even ourselves. Accountable individuals maintain transparency, seek honest and constructive feedback, and take ownership of the outcomes of their actions and decisions. They are responsible to themselves and others and refrain from actions which discredit themselves or our service.

Bob Marley's quote at the beginning of this passage defines the greatness of a person not by the wealth they accumulated but by their integrity and their ability to affect others around them positively. Former Prime Minister of the United Kingdom Tony Blair keeps us on track when he says, "Sometimes it is better to lose and do the right thing than to win and do the wrong thing."

Habit 1:
N IS FOR "NO"

"No": learn to say this word in an empowering manner. Establish your priorities and try not to compromise them because you felt pressure from your peers. Be aware of and prepared for the consequences when you do. – Peter Smith

The art of leadership is saying no, not saying yes. It is very easy to say yes. – Tony Blair

When we're young and eager to be accepted as part of a group or to be in with the cool crowd, it can be difficult to say no to the things we know are against our best interest; this is part of growing up. As we enter our young adult stage, however, it should be a high priority to begin practicing better habits, as the consequences for saying yes to the wrong things can escalate quickly the nearer we get to age eighteen. Many people feel that saying no is a challenge, but with time, patience, and practice anyone can become skilled in the art of making a no sound less judgmental, and so positively influence others around you—for example, "Hey Pete, let's grab some beers and knock down some mailboxes!" "Sorry, fellas. I'd join you, but I've got to head to swim practice and can't even afford to pay for my own mailbox, let alone my neighbor's." You're deflecting the peer pressure with an empowering no through subtle use of humor, and without saying, "Dudes, you're a bunch of idiots. Let's not, and say we did." The concept here is to understand that the demands on your time begin to increase as you enter the adult years. Learning to say no, not just regarding behavior but also in beginning to prioritize the use of your time, is a positive move. This is movement toward developing a solid learning foundation for the amount of information getting ready to be fire-hosed our way during our college and adult learning experiences. Determining our personal priorities for what we want to accomplish in sports, academics, or work during this stage of our lives will help us be confident every time we need to say no. It becomes easier with practice, especially when we discover that many of our peers are less offended by it than we expected.

Learning to say no boils down to establishing our own priorities instead of following those of others. We're deciding and acting intentionally in accordance with those priorities. Tony Blair spent 10 years as the Prime Minister of the United Kingdom leaving behind his legacy of experienced wisdom reminding us of the relationship between the art of leadership and saying no. Peer pressure is a tough contender: we want to be liked, accepted, and known as fun to hang around with, but not if the time cost for saying yes starts to affect our personal priorities. Our friends will still be there—and if not, we'll make more along our way.

"Priorities?" you say. "I'm too young. I don't have any priorities." You have more than you think. Studying, sports, music, play, work, volunteering—all of these activities require prioritization of time, or else we won't get the A, win against a tough team, play well in the recital, or get a bonus for a job well done. You just haven't thought of your dedication to these activities in terms of prioritization. If you start thinking in terms of how to "rack and stack" your time now, you'll be more efficient later. Learning to say no to going out today so that you can study for a biology test might mean time for an amazing date later—not a bad trade-off.

Virtue 2:
C IS FOR COMMITMENT

You can't know your true strengths, weaknesses, or abilities unless you warrior up and commit to getting in the arena. Fear is your mind and body in a heightened state of awareness. The courage to commit is fear's opponent. Participate, and you'll learn to manage fear. – Peter Smith

Courage is the most important of all the virtues, because without courage you can't practice any other virtue consistently. You can practice any virtue erratically, but nothing consistently without courage. – Maya Angelou

In fighter pilot–speak, "commit" is the command to engage our opponent until they or we disappear from the radar screen. Courageous and commitment go hand in hand, since the noun often requires the adjective in order to make the pledge or to commit to the undertaking. In my opinion, commitment is more worthy of discussion as a key virtue for young adult endeavors. Few people will argue that we live in an "instant gratification" culture today. Young adults tend to be courageous by nature but more fearful of the work or time commitments required to complete worthy causes. We are less tolerant of delaying gratification. Our patience for engaging in activities restricting freedom of action until completion are challenged by "get rich quick," "bigger, better deals," and "grass is greener" dreaming in the YouTube and Facebook syndrome. I'm not shaming these incredible media for the improvements they have brought. But I'm advocating we teach and learn to manage these contexts in a healthy, empowering way that's appropriate for each stage of life. It takes commitment to remain dedicated to a cause or to see an activity through to completion. We can't know or develop the knowledge of what something is like or whether or not we can do something unless we commit to doing it and seeing it through to its logical conclusion. Fear is human, and it's good for us. Fear will never go away. Committing to learning and doing things despite fear is where we begin creating our way. Courage gets us into the arena; commitment keeps us in it.

Many activities have interested us, but we don't check them out because of the fear of getting hurt, of not being able to afford it, of failing, of the unknown, of being laughed at or made fun of. This doesn't mean we should go out there and commit to doing dangerous things just for the sake of it! There are some things that look cool and extreme but don't pass our personal "courage of commitment" interest or desired experience.

We have to get up off the couch and try things. As Jedi Master Yoda said, "Do or do not: there is no try." If you think football looks like fun, get out and experience it. If you want to be able to say no to things to get your time back, practice it. You want to learn to free-dive and spearfish, but you're worried about drowning or sharks—so take swimming lessons and jump into the ocean to see for yourself. Most activities we view as exciting or challenging involve some sort of risk or consequence. We have to get comfortable with uncomfortable risk, or there will be no rewards. We don't want to be always on the sideline, saying, "That looks exciting!" We want to experience it ourselves—and this takes commitment. We get better at this virtue with practice. We may get bumped and bruised along the way, but we'll be stronger for the experience and know a lot more about what we can do, while also learning what we choose not to do.

Here I'd like to take a moment to share with parents and students some personal "courage of commitment" examples we experienced with our own children, to give more perspective on this virtue.

On a trip to Maine years ago, Jessy, our seven-year-old, looked on with wonder as her brothers and sister jumped from a 30-foot-high abandoned railroad trestle into the cool clear water below. Scary stuff for a little three-footer! But boy did those kids look like they were having fun climbing all over that thing and leaping off. She was definitely scared of the height, and I'll never forget when she grabbed my hand for me to take her up there to peek over the side, one foot well back, one toe over the side, her brothers and sister encouraging her to give it a try and they'd jump with her. A crowd gathered around to check out this crazy little kid thinking about jumping off the bridge. She moved forward, pulled back, moved forward and pulled back. "Jessy, you don't have to try this now," I told her. "We can climb down to where it's lower. Nobody expects you to jump from here. That's a high jump for a little person." And as I started to move away to take her lower over the side, she leaped when I least expected it, and I jumped in after her. She came up from the water grinning from ear to ear screeching with excitement as the crowd went wild. (I am thankful her mother wasn't there, or I wouldn't be writing this right now.) Was it unsafe? Was I a bad parent for letting her jump? She'd been a swimmer from six months old, so the swimming part was not a factor. I could see those gears turning, like she wanted to commit to trying it. I was probably more scared than she was, but this wasn't about me: it was about my child and her desire in that moment to enjoy what the other kids were enjoying, despite her youth and size. In this case, the reward far outweighed the risk. This small, courageous victory of committing to jump and managing her fear with Dad and siblings there to support or rescue her would go a long way in her development. Today she continues developing her confidence, courageously committing to challenging tasks. It's not a reckless courage to commit that she's developed—it's a calculated one. I'm not telling you to go find a 30-foot-high bridge and encourage your kid to jump into the water below; I'm sharing a "teachable moment" story we'll all face as parents, where we may have to set aside our own fears so our children can conquer theirs.

I remember when Cole, Jessy's older brother, was ten years old and committed to "manning up" as he apologized for being rough and unkind with our neighbor's daughter while playing kickball in our cul-de-sac. And I'll never forget the pride I felt as I watched Cole be his older brother Dean's wingman when Dean was falsely accused of using a neighbor child's scooter without her permission.

My wife and I got the whole family involved in the Israeli self-defense martial art of Krav Maga so our kids would be better prepared for any bullying at school. My oldest son, Dean, came home one day worried he was in trouble after pushing back against a kid who was bullying him during lunchtime. I was proud of him for committing to defend himself, and even prouder of the school for investigating the matter and rightfully disciplining the kid who was doing the bullying. Both kids moved on from the experience and learned from it.

When I was deployed, I enjoyed news my wife sent me about my oldest daughter, Erika, committing to publicly address a crowd at a Mayor's Youth Council event. I thought to myself, "It took me 30 years to be able to do something like that, and it can still be a frightening experience for me." The reason I emphasize commitment as a virtue is that committing to enter any unknown, uncertain arena where we have doubts and feel imperfect is an exercise in expanding our knowledge and managing fear. Being courageous itself does not imply action; commitment to trying to achieve or experience something does. It's a chicken-or-egg discussion. Regardless, as Maya Angelou suggested, courage is the keystone of all other virtues and an integral part of our process for committing to CREATEing our way.

Habit 2:

E IS FOR EGO

There are "Good, Bad, and Ugly" egos. Surround yourself with the good ones. Try not to take another's criticism of you personally, and don't compare yourself to them. Revel in and work with your universal uniqueness. – Peter Smith

We come nearest to the great when we are great in humility. – Rabindranath Tagore

Clint Eastwood starred in the Western film *The Good, the Bad, and the Ugly*. Eastwood was the "good," likable, calculated gunfighter of poetic justice; human, fallible, and in some ways not much better than the other two thugs, but he made good-over-evil choices. Teamed up with Clint was "the ugly," an expert gunfighting bandit who provides chicanery, stupidity, and comic relief, and makes ugly choices look easy. The third character is the solitary "bad" gunfighting bounty hunter, in the game only for himself and quite comfortable choosing evil. It's a nuanced portrayal of the human struggle.

When we're young we want the attention, we want the fame and fortune. Our egos want to be fed with validation, approval, reward, likeability, popularity. We may find ourselves hanging out with the wrong crowd in the interest of being perceived as cool. We may find ourselves willing to lie, cheat, or steal to get ahead, be at the top of the class, or seem like we are more courageous than we actually behaved. This is all part of growing up, and your parents, teachers, mentors, coaches, and peers get it. Now, however, as a young adult, it's a good time to be more aware of the ego and its pitfalls. When you turn eighteen, there are legal consequences for not learning to control your ego.

What is *ego*? Upon searching the internet's dictionary.com and Wikipedia, the following combination of words and sentences best defines a shared contextual mental model: It's the "I," the self of any person; the conscious subject; a person thinking, feeling, and willing, and distinguishing one's self from the selves of others and from objects of its thought. The psychoanalytic perspective describes ego as the part of the psychic apparatus that experiences and reacts to the outside world and thus mediates between the primitive drives of the id and the demands of the social and physical environment. Synonyms are self-esteem, self-image, feelings. "Your criticism wounded his ego." Ego is the complete person, both body and soul.

American capitalism has a tendency to highlight and reward big egos handsomely. One look at the magazine rack at the grocery checkout counter proves this. But these are exceptions, not the rule. Most famous and influential people who survive history and become classroom lessons for humanity had good egos, humble and considerate of other human beings: Abraham Lincoln, Harriet Tubman, the pope, Guatama Buddha, Mother Teresa, George Washington, Winston Churchill, Theodore Roosevelt, Princess Diana to name a few. Today, media and advertising have helped create a society where ego sells well. Good sales isn't necessarily a calling for anyone to continually seek ways to boost their image. In fact, boosting one's ego can be a risky endeavor if it involves malice or compromising one's integrity. Surrounding ourselves with good egos helps mitigate temptations to boost our own image for selling ourselves to others.

Speaking of others, whom am I referring to with "them" in my opening quote? Consider "them" your peers, critics, family, colleagues, teammates, society in general. We want to be aware of the ways in which we're being influenced in our thoughts and actions by what "they" think. We want to think and act from our own heart, not their heart. We want to be less concerned about what they think of me and more conscious of what I think of me. We want to receive criticism from them constructively, regardless how it is delivered.

What we're striving for here in our young adult years is to develop a healthy, balanced approach regarding our ego. We want to feel good about ourselves, but not at the expense of others. We need to be content with ourselves before we can enjoy others. Our young adult years are just the place to develop this love of self.

Rhonda Byrne's book *The Secret* looks at the law of attraction. This law applies to most aspects of our lives, in terms of intending the things you want and how the universe responds to your thought frequency. She's not the first to speak of this, but she does a great job explaining it. An easy way to visualize this is the phrase "you are what you eat." If your thoughts and actions revolve around the intake of fatty foods, then chances are you have attracted fat to your physical body. If your thoughts are about never getting ahead financially in life, then scarcity is what you'll attract versus abundance. I can easily let my ego control my behavior in negative ways and attract negative outcomes. Good egos are those that are unconcerned about what "they" think. Good egos choose to do the right thing despite potential boosts. Good egos are humble and don't boast or brag about their achievements. Good egos attract people, circumstances, and events into their lives that match what they intend to create for their lives. Bad egos, however, are willing to hurt others physically and emotionally to look better themselves—definitely to be avoided. Ugly egos are the in-between. These egos make careless choices and are carefree about the consequences, but they don't harm others. Ugly egos are willing to tell lies or cheat to look better, but not necessarily with intent to harm others, like a bad ego. Have you met good, bad, and ugly egos? Whom do you prefer to spend your time with? Do you identify yourself as bad or ugly? If so, can you alter your ego toward the good?

The U.S. military talks about "duty, honor, and country." The Air Force core values include "integrity first, service before self, and excellence in all we do." JetBlue's organizational core values are "safety, caring, integrity, passion, and fun." Every healthy organization has a set of core values intended to shape the working culture so all hands on deck will row in the same direction, be it sovereignty as a nation, winning wars, or earning profits. Imagine an age in which the majority of people put aside their egos for core values such as those expressed above—and in this excerpt from General Curtis E. LeMay:

I hope that the United States of America has not yet passed the peak of honor and beauty, and that our people can still sustain certain simple philosophies at which some miserable souls feel it incumbent to sneer. I refer to some of the Psalms, and to the Gettysburg Address, and the Scout Oath. I refer to the Lord's Prayer, and to that other oath which a man must take when he stands with hand uplifted and swears that he will defend his country. None of these words described, or the beliefs behind them, can be sung to modern music. But they are there, like rocks and oaks, structurally sound and proven. They are more than rocks and oaks; they are the wing and the prayer of the future. Whether we venture into the realms of space in our latest vehicles, or whether we are concerned principally with overhauling our engines and loading our ordnance here on the ground, we will still be part of a vast proud mechanism which must function cleanly if it is to function at all...Crank her up. Let's go.

The habit of surrounding ourselves with good egos as a young adult will set in motion a habit carrying us to adventures and experiences we may not have imagined. One of the first steps in developing the ability to get out of our own way is learning not to take what others have to say about us personally. "How do I do that?" you ask. Here are some tips. First, give the benefit of the doubt to the person critiquing you. Maybe they're joking, or maybe they're just having a bad day. Regardless, if they are personally attacking you, it's probably more about them than it is about you. So try to control your emotions. It's not easy, and our growing-up experience may determine how quickly we develop and improve this habit. When we feel attacked, we tend to focus not on what the person said but on how we feel. Unless we quickly move off the "feel" part and refocus on the other person, we can go down a path of anger, which never ends well. Focus on that person and how they treat others: teasing, insulting, or gossiping may be their modus operandi. Maybe that person is insecure, threatened by you. If so, don't feel bad for being your awesome self, but think of ways to make this person feel better. Remember when Mom and Dad told us, "You don't need anyone's approval." If someone doesn't like you or is unhappy with you, that doesn't mean you did anything wrong. And don't be afraid to speak up if you feel wronged, because maybe this type of treatment is how the person was raised and they've never realized they're saying hurtful things. When you do speak up, don't be aggressive; just let them know how you feel. Remember, too, that we don't want to take compliments from others too personally. We don't want to base our self-worth on what others have to say about us. Humility is a virtue that helps us maintain the balance between criticism and complement. Rabindranath Tagore reminds us *"We come nearest to the great when we are great in humility."* We'll talk more about this humility later. Next up in our discussion is *navigation*.

Habit 3:
N IS FOR NAVIGATE

Learn to thoroughly read a map of terrain, obstacles and all. Find your position on the map, orient yourself, and move to a position of higher ground somewhere in the distance. Achieving your goals is the same process. Remember, go from large to small identifying features that funnel you toward your target.
– Peter Smith

History is a guide to navigation in perilous times. History is who we are and why we are the way we are. – David C. McCullough

Until I understand where I am, I can't get to where I am going. This is the value of a compass when we are out walking or hiking and need to know we're going in the right direction. But we also have an internal North Star. It's that little nudge that tells us if we are on the right path to fulfilling our potential, or on the wrong path wasting energy traveling somewhere we don't need to go. So my advice to you is, pull out that compass every once in a while and make sure you are navigating in the right direction. – John C. Maxwell

Learning to navigate is one of the first things we're taught as a boy scout or girl scout, or a soldier, pilot, or sailor. The advent of technological wonders such as global positioning satellites and portable electronic devices that interface with those satellites has made it easier than ever before to navigate from one place to another. But being able to find where we are on planet Earth in relation to the sun, moon, stars, or geography around us, with the ability to plot location so we can move to a newly desired position, are life skills that will give us confidence in many facets of our young adulthood. The skills of finding where we are on a map, orienting ourselves to our surroundings, and charting a course around obstacles as we move toward our desired location are the same process for creating our way and achieving our dreams.

When I flew OV-10 Broncos and A-10 Warthogs back in the early 1990s, we didn't have GPS navigational systems to use for accurate navigation. We used to fly low to evade radar, and we used terrain masking to avoid surface-to-air missile systems. In order to find our way to the target, we flew with 1:250,000 (ratio of inches) and used 1:50,000 scale maps in the cockpit to fly to and pinpoint our targets. Our briefings would include extensive map study and plotting to determine the minimum-risk routes to the target area. These routes we would have to fly by holding up the map along our way, looking for the features from the map that we could identify while flying along at speeds of 275–375 miles per hour. Our motto was to find "big to small" features that funneled us toward the target area—for instance, a mountain peak taller than the others, where we could identify a valley to fly up or through, where we could pick up a river, stream, or creek leading to a point at which we could pop up and identify the target for engagement. Our cross-check mantra was to constantly scan "clock to map to ground," "head on a swivel, check wingman's six o'clock."

Developing a course of action for becoming a firefighter, doctor, lawyer, dentist, or any other profession is no different from flying low-level for 300 miles en route to a target. You have to identify the big things needed to lead you to the smaller, more precise target if you're going to become a medical doctor. You may want to take AP biology courses in high school, start looking at pre-med in college, get some intern experience to see what the job is really like, move on to medical school, internship, and doctorate. It's a map (remember the Da Vinci mind-mapping exercise). Along the way you'll encounter obstacles. You may get through pre-med and then discover that this path doesn't match who you are, which will require a change in course to an alternate target.

Navigation is a habit we want to develop in our young adult years. We want to learn to set a goal, chart a course toward achieving it, deviate around any obstacles, and end up at a logical conclusion of accepting that target or pursuing a different one. Our clarity exercise in the BOODA loop's observe and orient phases helped us recognize and determine our interest. Next, we decide and act on a course in which knowing or having a process for navigating brings us to the target. We may fail to reach the target for any number of reasons. That's not a problem; we adjust, observe, and start the loop over again, learning from our failures; we reorient ourselves to our interests; we decide and act all over again to reattempt or alter course. The best way to develop this habit is first to learn the fundamentals of reading a map. Find where you are on the map, orient with a compass, and practice navigating to a destination on foot without a GPS. Try for small navigational victories. Drive somewhere using a map instead of your smartphone. Look outside and find clues to the direction you're driving. Where is the sun? Why is there moss on one side of the tree? When you're confident in your ability to hike from A to B, charting a course for creating your way will start to look easy.

InCentivE$ is about helping design our inner compass for navigation. We're developing our "internal North Star," as John Maxwell suggests. Practice in "pulling out that compass," aligned to our "internal North Star," helps make orienting ourselves and CREATEing our way throughout the various stages of our lives flow naturally.

Habit 4:

T IS FOR TRIPLE TIMES

Take time to train yourself physically; you'll feel better. Take time to think about the world critically and draw your own conclusions. Take time to thank and develop an attitude of gratitude. – Peter Smith

I hated every minute of training, but I said, don't quit. Suffer now and live the rest of your life as a champion. – Muhammad Ali

Very little is needed to make a happy life; it is all within yourself, in your way of thinking. –Marcus Aurelius

Develop an attitude of gratitude, and give thanks for everything that happens to you, knowing that every step forward is a step toward achieving something bigger and better than your current situation. – Brian Tracy

We'll accomplish very little in life if we are unwilling to train ourselves to get better, learn, and achieve professional status. In his book *Outliers*, Malcolm Gladwell explained that achieving expertise or greatness in a particular skill averages out to 10,000 hours of practice. There are counterarguments critiquing Gladwell's 10,000 hours that focus on "nature versus nurture," IQ, and good coaching at a young age. But I think we can agree that the premise of this general rule is our music teacher's classic suggestion that "practice makes perfect." Training takes discipline. We can't make excuses, and laziness won't cut it. We either put in the time and the effort, or we expect mediocre results. Muhammad Ali didn't enjoy training, but the results were worth it. We're not going to make it in the big leagues by showing up every other game and only the practices we find convenient. We don't become doctors by watching YouTube videos. We have to train for it. We don't win in a merge with a MiG-29 unless we train for it. We don't get a physique like Arnold Schwarzenegger's by taking a couple days off from the gym. We don't become the next Kelly Slater of the world by turning down waves because the water is too cold.

Today's living standards often call for both Mom and Dad to work to earn a living. We're so busy, we let the kids decide if they want to play or not. We may want to be our kids' friends instead of their parents, letting them choose not to participate in the sports and activities that provide tremendous training environments for development through the young adult years. Physical education and free play are being replaced by video games, social media, and the fear of lawsuits over kids getting hurt on the playground. We need to create spaces for our children to take time to train and get better at something. We need this feedback to understand our capabilities. I like Wikipedia's definition of *training* as teaching, or developing in oneself or others, any skills and knowledge or fitness that relate to specific useful competencies (https://en.wikipedia.org/wiki/Training). The human mind and body are designed to be stretched. Get out there and stretch it! Take time to train it! We are wild by nature, so spend some time in it.

Thinking is extremely important, and it's especially relevant in our fast-paced world. We have to take time to think during our day and reflect on what went well—whether we stuck to our priorities, stayed on track regarding our focus or direction, assessed what's going on around us in the outside world—to maintain our situational awareness. What do I think of the news today? Did I question what was reported? Maybe I should check some other sources for the veracity of the subject and the credibility of the reporter or network. Is it possible that there is some salesmanship in what's being reported, or that what was reported went beyond the support of the emotional intelligence criterion. Was it editorialized, sensationalized, misleading? We need to know what *we* think about things, not what everybody else does. When we get lazy in our thinking, it becomes easy to latch onto the convenient thoughts or negativity expressed in the myriad of media streaming before us. Stop, look, and listen, and carve out some quiet, undistracted thinking time for yourself. Draw your own conclusions and challenge yourself to reframe negative thinking into positive action. Start by challenging yourself to counter one negative thought with two positive thoughts. Develop your personal mindfulness: purposely bringing your attention to the present moment without judging it, letting it pass and then identifying lessons learned from your daily experiences. Spend time in nature to feed your wild soul and think about where you're going.

The salient point behind taking "time to think" is getting ourselves out of the fog of all the distractions, expert opinions, media bias, celebrity gossip, political pandering, fearmongering, advertising programming, and conditioning. News sources are full of other people's views and rationales. Discover your own. Do the research; analyze and break things down into desired learning objectives (DLOs), focal points (FPs), contributing factors (CFs), root causes (RCs), and instructional fixes (IFs). This is how we brief and debrief our training missions flying fighter and attack aircraft. Before we fly an air combat mission against enemy adversaries, for example, we determine our mission objectives. "Our mission today is to detect, target, identify, sort, and kill all enemy airplanes en route to our target area, and to get our bombs on target on time." Our training missions typically incorporate tactical DLOs. When we've executed the mission and landed safely, we review our recorded performance and pick apart our DLOs. The DLOs are quantified and validated by identifying and defining key focal points (FPs), like "Why did I lose my wingman on the way to the target" or "Why didn't I achieve my desired weapons effects on my target?" "How did #3 successfully find his target and desired point of impact?" During the analysis of these focal points, we collectively debrief what we thought were the contributing factors of failure or success. Out of the contributing factors, we then agree upon and identify the root cause (RC) of the focal point. Once we have isolated the RC, then we come up with an instructional fix (IF) to prevent the focal point from detracting from our success the next time we conduct the mission. By completing this process each time, we discover our tactical weaknesses and strengths, helping us train to new DLOs. Such a process is easily adaptable to new information, experiences, what we hear, see, feel, and touch.

A quick example: Politician X says healthcare should be an entitlement because Y. Our DLO is why X believes in Y. Our FPs could be "What is candidate X's party?" There may be CFs of party affiliation that influence Politician X's belief in Y. There may be an RC in party affiliation for politician X's Y. Another FP could be "Politician X receives campaign contributions from healthcare company Y." This may be a CF to his or her view. This approach to news and information is the critical thinking component that the secondary education environment works to train and discipline young adults to do; but it needs reinforcement at home.

We can see that being constantly plugged in to entertainment easily leads us to think the way others want us to think if we don't take the time to critically think about it ourselves. We need to beware of the corporatization of America. It's much easier to analyze information critically if we have a habitual process to break it down—like DLOs, FPs, CFs, RCs, and IFs. There's nothing wrong with being entertained, and not everything requires analysis. There are many interesting and different points of view. But take a breath every now and then and take time to think for yourself. As Marcus Aurelius suggests to us, "Very little is needed to make a happy life; it is all within yourself, in your way of thinking."

Take time to thank, too. Brian Tracy's, "Develop an attitude of gratitude" quote at the beginning of this chapter outlines the benefits clearly. It's become cliché to pursue an "attitude of gratitude," but it's important. An attitude of gratitude is our ticket to humility and an avalanche of support from our parents, mentors, teachers, coaches, and peers. When we're grateful, we change how we think and feel, moving from lemons to lemonade, from negative to positive. This is not a "Pollyanna" viewpoint; rather, I'm suggesting that if we cultivate the habit of exercising gratitude each day, we begin processing events in such a way as creates general happiness and well-being. Remember Rhonda Byrne's *The Secret* and the law of attraction that we mentioned earlier? Gratitude is the first step in attracting to you the people, circumstances, and events for creating the life you want. Expressing gratitude takes practice. We live in a media storm of negativity and sensationalism, and we have to practice developing a habit of gratitude in this cultural environment. The first step in practicing gratitude is: don't take anything for granted. One of the benefits of military experience is stepping out of one's comfort zone. Having had the experience of living and traveling abroad, I've seen how good we have it here. Restaurants, theaters and entertainment, schools, roads, infrastructure, mass transit, jobs, housing, convenience stores and gas stations, hobbies, sports, playgrounds, parks, playtime—the list goes on and on. Do we think in these terms? Probably not, because of our perspective on the good things I just mentioned. "Doesn't everybody have these things?" This is our base standard in the U.S. We don't think in terms of not having reliable, clean water; of having to hike to the bathroom, toilets we have to clean ourselves; of using tarps for roofs. Get up in the morning and be grateful we got another day. Forget grumbling about school, homework, tests, and college admissions. Start out each day with thankfulness for the blessing of getting to experience those things, and before you know it, they won't seem so bad. The teachers who didn't much care about your flippant attitude will start to notice your good attitude—and suddenly their wealth of knowledge and experience becomes something that helps you. So let's learn to take time to thank in our daily lives. Gratitude is contagious. Giving up our seat on the crowded bus for someone else is gracious. Moving over to the left lane to let oncoming traffic merge safely is gracious. Picking up the trash in front of us instead of walking past it is taking time to thank.

Before we leave the "triple times," I want you to focus on the two words preceding the recommendation: *take* and *time*. "Take" implies action. We must commit to act on these recommendations. You'll have to be proactive about balancing these three *time* actions and scheduling them into your habitual patterns. Time is defined by man, not the universe. The universe doesn't care about time. We have divided time into 24 hours a day for everybody. Choose to use your limited amount of time on this planet wisely, productively, presently, and joyfully. Taking time implies deliberate action to set aside a portion of our hours each day to train ourselves physically, mentally, and spiritually to become better humans; to think reflectively, critically, resourcefully about our experiences, learning, and training; to express thanks to somebody or for something. "But I'm too busy to take time to train, time to think, time to thank." Really? I challenge young adults to carve out an hour a day to train physically, mentally, spiritually. Physically, carve out 45 minutes a day: 20–30 minutes of vigorous exercise, and 10–25 minutes to travel and get changed. If your gym is more than ten minutes from where you live, it's too far, so run in place and learn how to create a home gym, with sit-ups, push-ups, dips, stairs, and the great outdoors. If you have the ability to unplug during this time, you might be able to combine this process with taking time to think. Mentally, tune into your body and thoughts after your physical training. Get quiet for ten minutes and become aware of how you feel and whether or not your frame of mind is positive, negative, or worried. Accept the thoughts and feelings you are experiencing. Be aware of those thoughts and feelings as you take five minutes to feed your soul with something spiritual: a great story of human compassion; uplifting quotes; motivational speeches or sayings; a religious book; a good podcast. This hour of physical, mental, and spiritual training is a way to become more emotionally intelligent in our fast-paced world with all its demands.

So we're taking an hour each day to train, mentally, physically, and spiritually. Now let's take ten minutes a day to listen to what's going on in the world and think about it critically. Look through a few headlines, check the sources, verify credibility, and form your thoughts and opinions. Doing this will teach you to seek to understand before being understood; far too many of us speak before we've actually listened or understood. We can look forward to great respect from our peers, colleagues, and coworkers as we develop this ability to seek to understand before being understood.

Take five minutes a day to be thankful. We didn't get where we are without the help of others. Everyone is connected to others in gratitude. If you don't think so, then consider the jeans you're wearing. First, you're a young adult and probably don't have a job, and so your mom, dad, or other relative bought them for you. Thank them. Second, if we're lucky, those jeans were made here in America by someone who ensured that the fabric was correctly loaded into the assembly and that the right buttons were pushed in the factory to create the great garment you're now wearing. Thank them. Third, somebody designed them for you. Thank them. Fourth, some farmer got up at oh-dark-thirty to make sure the tractor was ready to comb the cotton from the field, which eventually went into your jeans. I could go on about how we are all connected and intertwined. There is always somebody or something we can be thankful for. These five minutes of your day will humble you.

In total, we are talking about an hour and fifteen minutes of your 24-hour day. Mix, match, move around, increase, decrease—what matters is not the amount of time you dedicate to these three disciplines but the habit of including them in your daily routine. If you develop the daily habit of these disciplines, you will recover hours of productivity within your day. I'm certain of that. However, don't confuse my recommendation with the need to be productive throughout the day. Take time to relax, play, and enjoy. It's OK to do nothing some days. But it's not OK to do nothing when we are able, and when we expect others to expend their own resources to care for you. We all have to participate. "Teamwork makes the dream work!" (Yes, I said it; cringe if you must.)

Habit 5:
I IS FOR INFORM YOURSELF

Maintain a desire to learn throughout your life. Actively listen to others and strive to understand before you talk. – Peter Smith

A public opinion poll is no substitute for thought. – Warren Buffett

There is a difference between "time to think" and "I is for Informing ourselves." "Time to think" was all about the breakdown of information, framed in a process to help us critically analyze. Habit 5, on the other hand, is all about feeding ourselves information for understanding and knowledge. The more knowledge we have, the easier it becomes to take time to think.

On the way to Mitchell Hall (the chow hall) at the Air Force Academy, we passed by an eagle-and-fledgling statue, with the quote, "Man's flight through life is sustained by the power of his knowledge." That gave us motivation to learn, as we made our way from food in Mitchell to thought in our classrooms. Have we had enough of the experts on TV yet? When we research the self-proclaimed experts addressing us through the media channels, we often find out that the person advising us has little experience in the field—maybe less than we do ourselves—yet is presented to us as the expert. The sales and corporatization of the media have millions of people falling for their word as gospel, without doing our own research. I encourage you to do your own homework. Verify the experts' credibility and question the media source's agenda. I'm not advocating that young adults become cynics. Instead, I'm encouraging you to "trust, but verify."

Don Miguel Ruiz is the author of *The Four Agreements: A Toltec Wisdom Book*. The essence I pulled from reading his book was guidance toward happier living by recommending that we seek to understand others before we ourselves are understood. My key takeaway from reading his description of the agreements is for us to learn more about people, their background, upbringing, culture, religion, environment, political affiliation, and family before we think we accurately understand the information the individual is conveying. Once we have sought to understand the person, then we ourselves are better informed and better positioned to be understood. This is true of the media or any entity conveying advice, guidance, position, or information. Do your own homework. Seek out the resources, which have never been more accessible than today.

Again, I is for informing ourselves. Read, study, and seek to understand before talking back. Don't rely on one source for information, but use many; compare and contrast, and take time to think about the information. Practicing this habit will help us learn to listen more actively.

"What does active listening mean?" We are so distracted by speed, convenience, social media, and smartphones that we've developed into poor listeners with short attention spans. In a sense, we've all become boring compared to the entertainment we can get from the 4x6 inch electronic device in our hands. Telephone companies and internet service providers love it. When was the last time you remembered someone's name after they introduced themselves? We need to be present in the moment and actively listen. The easiest way to improve our listening skills actively is to pay attention in the moment and be aware that there is nothing more important than what this person has to share with us right now. There will be an opportunity to engage or escape later, but right now we need to give this person respect as a fellow human being, since we also want to be heard. We can listen, get their name, ask questions about their lives, or tell them it was a pleasure to meet them. If we have pressing matters to attend to, we can repeat their name and ask forgiveness for not being able to give them the attention they deserve at that moment—maybe we can arrange another, less distracted, time? Let's start listening so we can weed out the nonsense from the good sense. The more distracted we are, the easier it is for other people to take advantage of us.

Habit 6:
V IS FOR VISUALIZE

Intention is picturing in your mind how the achievement of your goal tastes, smells, and feels. This intention will naturally bring you to the people, circumstances, and events necessary to realize your vision. – Peter Smith, crafted and paraphrased from leadership and spiritual guru lessons of Wayne Dyer, John Maxwell, Jack Canfield, Bob Proctor, Lisa Nichols, and Rhonda Byrne

Vision animates, inspires, transforms purpose into action. – Warren G. Bennis

A master in the art of living draws no sharp distinction between his work and his play, his labor and his leisure, his mind and his body, his education and his recreation. He hardly knows which is which. He simply pursues his vision of excellence through whatever he is doing and leaves others to determine whether he is working or playing. To himself he always seems to be doing both. Enough for him that he does it well. – L. P. Jacks

"V is for Visualize" is a critical habit for the young adult stage of life. Books have been written just on the topic of visualization. So my challenge to you is to take this complex topic and condense it into a simple, executable habit that doesn't require years of quiet meditation in a mountaintop temple.

During my time as an admissions liaison officer, advising high school juniors and seniors about the path to ROTC and service academy admission, I had the opportunity to speak in the classroom on many career days. I would often ask, "What are your plans after high school?" The answers were mostly predictable: go to college, join the military, work. Sometimes I would get very specific answers, like, "I'm going to be a DKNY model," or "I'm going to be the next Tiger Woods," or "I'm going to play professional sports." I posed the question to start a dialog with the class about the difference between *fantasizing* and *visualizing*. I tried to explain to the students that both are important to the human condition, but they are different. The best way to demonstrate this difference was to delve further into students' post–high school plans. I would ask a student to join me in playing out their plans in a road-map sort of way. The young adult who wanted to be a DKNY model would have to take modeling classes, maintain a strict diet, be a certain height, and maintain marketable physical features. The young adult who wanted to be the next Tiger Woods would receive an education on muscle memory—and the fact that Woods was swinging a golf club at age three and winning tournaments before age ten with the 10,000 hours of muscle memory already ingrained. Michael Jordan may have initially been turned down by his high school basketball coach, but then he decided to make 300 free throws a day. Actually, he didn't shoot just 300 free throws a day; he took enough shots to make 300 free throws a day until developing the attitude and work regimen to become one of the most recognized and famous basketball champions of all time. Walter Peyton's off-season dedication to being the best running back in professional football was as intense as his on-season. Fantasy is the faculty or activity of imagining things, especially things that are impossible or improbable. Nobody wants impossible or improbable for our young adults. Dreams move from fantasy to reality when they meet with action. Fantasy plus action requires visualization. Instead of just watching the show, your mind, body, and spirit begin to participate intentionally to make the dream a reality. When we intend to do something, we are involving our senses. We start seeing ourselves as a professional basketball player. We seek out relationships and instruction, spending hours of the day on the court with coaches, studying plays, practicing drills, improving our dribbling, footwork, passing skills, jump shots, threes. We start to feel like a pro, sweat, smell like a pro, and experience the discipline of becoming a pro. The fantasy of becoming a professional basketball player ends when it connects with the vision and commitment to pursue all the elements required of a pro. Fantasy is improbable. Vision is definable, actionable, achievable, intentional. Warren G. Bennis tells us, "Vision animates, inspires, transforms purpose into action." So, when the students told me their plans, I forced them to think in terms of vision versus fantasy. Wishing it to be so is one thing; making it so is another. When you intend to do something, you will naturally attract to you the people, circumstances, and events to make your vision real, as we learned from *The Secret* by Rhonda Byrne. Before advancing to our next chapter, let's reread L. P. Jack's quote listed in the beginning of this chapter regarding mastering the art of living:

A master in the art of living draws no sharp distinction between his work and his play, his labor and his leisure, his mind and his body, his education and his recreation. He hardly knows which is which. He simply pursues his vision of excellence through whatever he is doing and leaves others to determine whether he is working or playing. To himself he always seems to be doing both. Enough for him that he does it well.

Virtue 3:
E IS FOR EXAMPLE

———————————————

Whatever you are asked to do or choose to do for yourself in work, study, sport or play is worth giving your best effort. Set a positive, inspiring example. – Peter Smith

A return to first principles in a republic is sometimes caused by the simple virtues of one man. His good example has such an influence that the good men strive to imitate him, and the wicked are ashamed to lead a life so contrary to his example. – Niccolò Machiavelli

Our government...teaches the whole people by its example. If the government becomes the lawbreaker, it breeds contempt for law; it invites every man to become a law unto himself; it invites anarchy. – Louis D. Brandeis (U.S. Supreme Court Justice, 1916–1939)

I can't remember how many times my grandmother said to me, "If somebody asks you to sweep the floor, sweep it like it was never swept before." I'm certain my Nonna got her advice from Dr. Martin Luther King's speech, and I recommend that you take three minutes to enjoy it here: https://www.youtube.com/watch?v=cZiN8gMHs64. My father and mother often told me that if I borrow something from someone, I should return it in better condition than when I borrowed it. They were teaching me to set a positive example. They knew how the real world works. If I complained about sweeping the floor and did a lousy job, then I would probably end up losing the job. If I mishandled things, borrowed or returned them in poor condition, I wouldn't get to use them again. By teaching me to set a positive example in all I was asked to do or chose to do, my parents were conditioning me to develop a good reputation. The real world talks. Your reputation will precede you—especially today, with an electronic footprint. When I was a kid, we didn't have to worry about social media or false attempts to tarnish our reputation due to malicious intentions, or bad or ugly egos. It's even more important today for us to put our best foot forward. And we don't need to be famous or powerful to set a positive example. Paraphrasing Niccolò Machiavelli's quote above, "One man's virtue is enough to shame the wicked into leading a life contrary to his example."

Look around our society. How are we doing? Are we setting positive examples? It seems that we hear more stories of politicians, celebrities, corporate executives, and athletes lying, cheating, and stealing than about those who are positively serving humanity. Part of this has to do with the media and our cultural preference for bad news, but this isn't good for us. We have to ask if our disgust with bad behavior is uniting us or angering us, making us culturally indifferent. Maybe we just like bad behavior. We certainly glamorize it on TV. What if we spent more time glamorizing the positive examples in our country? Would we be bored? Sure, we'll continue highlighting the bad behavior examples, but let's spend an equal amount of time with good behavior. We consumers wield a lot of power if we unite. We can turn it off, unfollow, dislike, unsubscribe.

We're a country of tremendously creative people with a government that's tolerant of expression. We work with some fabulously wealthy corporations. Certainly we can develop marketing campaigns, infomercials, and community campaigns that highlight our collective American examples of rude and inhumane behavior humorously, to encourage better behavior. I know it will be good for business and great for our American culture if we do. We can improve. We need to get back to work setting good examples in our country. Be the *ICE* men and *ICE* women warriors who do so. Speaking of warriors: an excellent example for us to strive is presented in Jack Hawley's

The Bhagavad Gita: A Walkthrough for Westerners (2001), where Hawley interprets the Hindu scripture and states, "For a warrior, war against evil, greed, cruelty, hate and jealousy is the highest duty" (17).1

Louis Brandeis was appointed to the Supreme Court on June 5, 1916: the first Jewish judge on our high court, known as the "people's attorney." He was a critic of big business and finance, particularly their interest in low wages and long hours. He was mistrustful of unlimited exercise of government power. I see a future of *ICE* men and women who think critically about today's big business and our government's role in our lives, keenly aware of Louis Brandeis work—and his intent in his quote above that encourages our government to set a positive example. Be the *ICE* men and *ICE* women who ensure that we don't swing our progressive pendulum back to a time before the positive American progress he helped bring about by serving in our high court.

1   Jack Hawley, *The Bhagavad Gita: A Walkthrough for Westerners* (Novato, California: New World Library, 2011).

Habit 7:
$ IS FOR $EN¢E OF HUMOR

Find the humor in life's adversities. You'll make mistakes. Get over it and forgive yourself. Experience the joy of being less serious, able to laugh at yourself along your way. Serving others will teach you humility. Remain humble and treat money as the result of your journey, not its purpose. – Peter Smith

If I had no sense of humor, I would long ago have committed suicide. – Mahatma Ghandi

One of the things that binds us as a family is a shared sense of humor. – Ralph Fiennes

A person without a sense of humor is like a wagon without springs. It's jolted by every pebble on the road. – Henry Ward Beecher

Our American socioeconomics and demographics condition us for stress. We feel stress about politics, education, business, jobs, status, earning a living, providing for our families, and budgeting for vacations, all while trying to balance our time off to enjoy our lives a bit. Life has become easier for all of us in terms of conveniences, but our wages haven't kept up with the cost of living. So we fill the time savings with increased productivity to earn more money, taking away the benefits of the time-saving conveniences. This is unsustainable, and tiresome, conditioning us for cynicism and indifference. We don't want this for ourselves or our families, which requires of us a strong $en¢e of humor about the role money will play in our lives and our individual ability to manage its relevance.

My use of the $ sign instead of the letter S is purposeful. Money is important, and there's no use minimizing its role for our living conditions. However, we often construct our lives with money in mind first, never considering whether we're earning it in alignment with our "who" and our "what." This is why we talk about it last. We have a better chance of earning money in alignment with our interests if we develop and understand *ourselves* first. The road to earning money can get bumpy, which is where a "$en¢e of humor" comes into play.

Developing our $en¢e of humor manages stress and helps us develop lifestyle expectations in balance with the associated costs. It would be great if we could get back to relaxing a little, not taking ourselves so seriously: getting out and hitting a few balls on the golf course, bowling with guardrails, running on the beach, going on hikes, playing Frisbee in the cul-de-sac with our neighbors. Our culture emphasizes material motivational priorities at the expense of our spiritual health. We can be deliberate about combating this by developing better consumer and lifestyle habits. The days of carrying clubs, living in caves, and hunting and gathering have given way to our need for money. I'm not minimizing money's importance in our society. Financial stress is not fun. But we can do a better job educating ourselves and our youth about money. We need to get ahead of it by incorporating financial education in our homes if we can't get it into our schools. Young adults who are financially educated will move on to provide strong future leadership in our corporations, designing pay and compensation benefits that align with net disposable incomes. Our young adult years are an excellent training ground for developing a $en¢e of humor in building financially wise foundations, before the costs of housing, children, student debt, and other responsibilities creep into our lives. There are a plethora of podcasts and online learning tools for developing our financial education. Our cultural secondary educational paradigm of reading, writing and arithmetic has not quite shifted to the inclusion of financial education. Our technological revolution is changing this paradigm rapidly. In the meantime, I've posted some examples for young adults to get started with financial literacy on my website combatstinkythinking.com.

Reframing our young adult thinking in terms of treating money as the result of our journey, not its purpose, lends itself to mindfulness about our creative choices. We are much happier adults when the money we earn is the result of what we most enjoy doing. I understand there are realistic challenges to this way of thinking, and sometimes getting the money first allows you to do the things you enjoy later. There are always exceptions. But I bet if we align ourselves with being inspired by "What is meaningful for me?" instead of "What's in it for me?" during our young adult years, we will experience more joy—and money—in our adult years. The dollar and cent signs in "$en¢e of humor" are a reminder to young adults to keep money considerations for our journey last, not first, when executing your BOODA loop. Try to maintain your $en¢e of humor, whether you earn a large or small amount of money along the way. Remember, the traditional ways of earning money are rapidly changing. Never in history has there been so much opportunity to earn a living doing what we enjoy. *InCentivE$* for CREATEing our way is a process for developing our characters first, and the money will follow.

There is no question that we're jumping into the world of uncharted territory as young adults creating our way. We are surrounded by influence, challenge, expectation, doubt, fear, failure, success, curiosity, envy, joy, sadness, love, fun, work, play, professors, employers, colleagues, opponents, competitors, and friends. There's no shortage of obstacles to navigate while creating our way. As Ghandi suggests, these obstacles are best met with a good $en¢e of humor and the ability to navigate around, over, or through them. Ghandi clearly hints at these obstacles in his quote: "If I had no sense of humor, I would long ago have committed suicide." Having and developing our sense of humor doesn't mean we should be able to tell jokes and make people laugh all the time. We can enjoy a sense of humor without being labeled a comedian. We can also be working professionals and maintain a sense of humor. The point is not to take life so seriously that we can't have fun with the adversities we encounter along the way. As young adults vying for our place in the world, we're going to get bumps and bruises—as Henry Ward Beecher reminds us, "A person without a sense of humor is like a wagon without springs. It's jolted by every pebble on the road." If we let those bumps and bruises harm our sense of self, we'll have difficulty bouncing back. There are few limits the world will offer us that we can't find joy in participating in. Our joy will require discovery and will be found sooner if we have the ability to laugh and not take ourselves too seriously during our journey. We will make mistakes. If we learn to laugh at ourselves, then we can learn from our mistakes, forgive ourselves, and move forward. Our $en¢e of humor can be developed by listening to funny people, podcasts, and shows, or by reading humorous books. The more we see the lighter side of things, the better able we'll be to develop this characteristic in ourselves and our families.

I enjoy Ralph Fiennes's quote: "One of the things that binds us as a family is a shared sense of humor." Fiennes is expressing the wisdom he's learned regarding the power of a good sense of humor to keep families together. We are all flawed, and many of us have family members we believe are so flawed that we roll our eyes and shake our heads when we think about them. Laugh with them. Seek to understand and accept them for who they are. Be a family, stick together, be loyal, and remember the old adage, "Blood is thicker than water." Let's not let silly disagreements keep any seats empty at the Thanksgiving table. Strong families make for strong nations. We have to defend mindfully and consciously against the "grass is greener" Hollywood, tabloid, and social media glamorization. Polarizing politics, media sensationalism, social justice, fake news, inequality, and student debt are just some of the issues that seem to be dividing us more than uniting us. It is going to take a new generation of young adult *ICE* men and *ICE* women with good senses of humor to correct our course. I'm confident that your generation will step up to the plate and improve our batting average.

Humor and humility are closely related. Improving our batting average requires that we serve others. We don't thrive on an island. We don't improve our lives in a vacuum. We help each other to make our families healthy, our nations great, and our corporations profitable. Serving others teaches us humility. Many of us do not have a proper "$en¢e" of our privileges, because we have not ventured outside our bubbles to experience or serve those with less. Volunteer to help nonprofits, the homeless, the elderly, disabled veterans, foster children, or the physically challenged for perspective and empathy. The honor in doing so gives us perspective and individual power to prevail and progress. We experience grace. We see how connected we are through this service. Put the spiritual before the material.

Together we've covered *InCentivE$*, a tool for developing our emotional intelligence (EI). Next stop on our **CREATE** checklist is A, for us to consider how we can "Add value" to others in developing our post–high school game plan.

CHAPTER 5:

A is for Adding Value

When you live your life in alignment with a purpose that is centered on selflessly adding value for others, opportunities become abundant, and your life becomes fulfilled. – Hal Elrod

Money is one of the rewards you get for adding value to the lives of others. – Paul McKenna

How can we improve upon our interests and talents to add value to other's lives? This is an excellent question to keep in mind while BOODA-looping your way through class and practicing the *InCentivE$* virtues and habits. Adding value to mine and other people's lives is an excellent framework for motivation to continue the creative process to a logical conclusion of pass, fail, do over, revamp, or abandon for an alternative course.

Getting used to the concept of adding value will follow us through our entire lives as a business owner, employer, employee, team member, husband, wife, brother, sister, son, or daughter. Adding value scales across the entire spectrum of our lives. How can I add value to my relationships, my job, my team, neighbors, friends, coworkers? Hal Elrod's quote in the beginning of this chapter succinctly summarizes how living our lives in alignment with a purpose centered on "selflessly adding value for others" will create abundant opportunities along our journey leading to fulfilling lives. I agree. We can get started now as we CREATE our post–high school game plans.

We don't need to complicate the meaning of adding value. I've seen whole books written on the subject, applying the concept to conversation, specific relations, diplomacy, business, service, negotiations, and more. We know in our hearts and minds how to add value to any situation by how it feels. We know this feeling maintains a separate value existence in our lives in addition to money, as conveyed in Paul McKenna's quote, "Money is one of the rewards." If those we intend to work with, serve, or influence feel good about our input, our additions or subtractions to a given situation, then we are most likely adding value. We may have not thought in terms of our personality, attitude, or actions as bringing value to the table, but adolescence is a great time to start. Our young adult years are typically framed in the context of maturity, growth, and learning. "How do I add value?" is not a typical classroom question. It's more typical of a post-collegiate interview or on-the-job, scenario-based training exercise. But we can start asking ourselves "add value" questions earlier, before we graduate high school.

Ask what talents you bring to the team; what skills you possess that translate into something others may need or are not good at doing themselves; which characteristics you have that your team or another team could use? Are you inventive? Tenacious? Do you like to stand up or stand out? Maybe you like to get things done, or ponder how to get things done more efficiently. You may be a doer or an innovator, bringing a sense of wonder to the team. Perhaps you're a galvanizer. What is a galvanizer, you ask? A galvanizer is a leader who collects people's input when assessing challenging situations bringing them together to stimulate thought and excitedly influencing everyone toward the win, progress or solution to a problem. Use *InCentivE$* and the BOODA loop as guides to discover the value you can add. Taking *InCentivE$* as our character backdrop while exercising our personal BOODA loops, it's hard for me to imagine a situation in life which we won't instinctively respond in a manner consistent with adding value.

CHAPTER 6:

T is for Tenacity

Many of life's failures are people who did not realize how close they were to success when they gave up. – Thomas Edison

Real courage is when you know you're licked before you begin, but you begin anyway and see it through no matter what. – Harper Lee (from *To Kill a Mockingbird*)

The context of the definition of tenacity I'm using for our checklist is best exemplified by the quotes above. Dictionaries define tenacity as the quality or state of being determined, continuing to exist, persistence. This characteristic is important in today's highly distracting environment with shorter attention spans. We are conditioned for instant gratification in an environment of informational overload. We need a process for filtering all this information, as we discussed with our BOODA loop. Bringing the BOODA loop into a learning environment helps us remain present and attentive. Being oriented around our *InCentivE$* virtues and habits frames our thinking, approach, and attitude to subject matter or daily activity. What remains is for us to put it together and do the work to see our vision through to logical conclusions and intended destinations. When we arrive, we assess whether we passed, failed, or need to redo—but we don't give up in the middle of the looping process because of difficulties or obstacles. We navigate the obstacle until we reach a logical conclusion or our intended destination. Should we discover that the destination does not fulfill our intended vision, we start the loop over with new observations. Now we have a new focal point from which to instructionally fix or adjust. Tenacity completes the loop, gets the job done or brings us to a branching point. Tenacity is our work ethic, our resisting the temptation to give up at the first sign of not being gratified. There is such a thing as delayed gratification, which our culture and many of us don't give ourselves the time, patience, or effort to discover, as Thomas Edison so eloquently suggests.

Harper Lee, in her classic novel *To Kill a Mockingbird*, told us something similar. Many college students go home after their freshman year or change their majors multiple times because a class becomes too difficult and turns them off, only to wish later that they had seen it through. Even if we end up at the wrong destination after completing our major, or the vision is not what we intended when completed, we will have learned something from the process of seeing it through. This is tenacity. When we discover halfway through our accounting major we can no longer see ourselves working asset and liability spreadsheets or doing other people's taxes, we learn a lot about ourselves by finishing the bachelor's degree anyway. There is a myriad of ways to pivot from this degree in a meaningful way in our workforce. There are numerous mentoring "been there, done that" resources to show us how. What we learn by seeing it through, we now insert into our bag of tricks for our next endeavor.

Despite the overwhelming odds of being licked by Deep South prejudice and inequality, Harper Lee's Atticus Finch has the courage to take on and tenaciously fight racial injustice and the destruction of innocence. Her fictional character serves as a moral hero to all of us and an example of tenacious integrity for all. Seeing it through is never time wasted. Be tenacious!

CHAPTER 7:

E is for Enthusiasm

A man can succeed at almost anything for which he has unlimited enthusiasm. – Charles Schwab

Success consists of going from failure to failure without loss of enthusiasm. – Winston Churchill

There is a certain enthusiasm in liberty, that makes human nature rise above itself, in acts of bravery and heroism. – Alexander Hamilton

The best definition I could find for "enthusiasm" is from the dictionary. cambridge.org entry, which describes enthusiasm as a feeling of energetic interest in a particular subject or activity and an eagerness to be involved in it. I was fortunate to have my first look at enthusiasm in a book my grandmother asked me to read: Norman Vincent Peale's *Enthusiasm Makes the Difference*. I had read the book before attending the U.S. Air Force Academy, which helped me remain enthusiastic through all of our experiences, courses, and training exercises. Over the years of my professional military career development, I've read countless authors who include enthusiasm in their teaching on leadership. Enthusiasm is unconditional. There are no prerequisites or circumstances for us to have it. It costs nothing, yet it has the potential of making all the difference in benefiting us in every aspect of our lives.

If you look up Norman Vincent Peale on Wikipedia, you'll find that his work models association with our post-revolutionary and Civil War American historical values of optimism and service. He is also the author of *The Power of Positive Thinking*. This is a man who lived through WWI, the great depression, WWII, the Korean War, our civil rights movements, Vietnam, the Cold War, and Desert Storm, and witnessed our transition from the industrial to technological innovation age. Peale dedicated his book to his grandchildren, which is probably one of the contributing factors for my grandmother giving the book to me. Both my Nonnas, as we lovingly called them, were enthusiastic, positive forces in our family despite having endured much adversity. I'm not suggesting we be enthusiastic in our response to every negative event life bestows upon us, and neither was Peale. What Peale was intending for us readers was not to fall prey to any cultural mediocrity trappings of humdrum status quo. Peale wanted everybody to become the best version of themselves, unleashing their creative forces and rising to their fullest potential. He wrote an entire book about enthusiasm making the difference between success and failure. We are fortunate to live in a country providing the structure and freedom to rise to our fullest potential. Today we may be familiar with the phrase "everybody gets a trophy," ensuring that all participants are recognized. This is a valid example of culturally appropriating mediocrity. This kind of trapping potentially saps individual enthusiasm with a feeling as if our positive investment of time and energy creates little difference in the outcome of our lives. This simply is not true and ought to be heavily defended against. Zest for life, pep in our step, and enthusiasm in our endeavors is not a difficult ask nor a difficult task that will be rewarded in feelings or achievement, if not in cash.

I love Charles Schwab's quote at the beginning of this chapter. Peale mentions Schwab's quote in his book about enthusiasm. Advertising has ensured that many young adults today are familiar with the financial services company bearing his name. Despite dyslexia, a poor upbringing and a distaste for self serving, crony enriching Wall Street brokers at the time, Charles Schwab's enthusiasm to make stock market trade participation affordable for the common man made his company a dynamic facilitator of wealth creation for countless Americans. He is one enthusiastic businessman.

Winston Churchill enthusiastically inspired his war-wearied Britons to remain vigilant in their fight against German fascism during WWII. He defines success for us in terms of enthusiastically progressing despite failure.

Alexander Hamilton invites us to reflect upon how liberty inspires enthusiasm in human nature to rise above itself in acts of bravery and heroism. This is close to the American values of optimism and service which Peale supported in his work.

Enthusiasm represents the last step of our CREATE checklist. This completes our journey together discussing the *InCentivE$* for CREATEing our way process. The following chapters of this book summarize our journey together and complete my accident's story with my rescue and my personal near-death testimony. Before we delve into these chapters, let's review how far we've come.

CHAPTER 8 | SUMMARY

We began this journey together learning about my accident as I introduced myself and my inspiration to write down guidance for my own children. We talked about how to execute John Boyd's OODA loop for discovering *Clarity*. We added a *B* to his loop to combat our twenty-first century propensity for instant gratification, and overwhelming information. The *B* reminds us to minimize distractions by *Being present* when exercising his loop. We understand now the practicality of developing *Relationships* with people to help manifest our way. We discussed how *Emotional intelligence* is more valuable to our growth and discovery than IQ (smarts) while creating our way. We spent a good portion of our reading travels putting the spiritual before the material redefining our *InCentivE$*, an acronym characterized by three virtues to strive for and roughly seven habits to practice in developing our emotional intelligence. We advocated thinking in terms of *Adding value* to others' lives through the gift of our personal interests and skills. We talked about how the entire process for CREATEing our way is iterative, lengthy, and will require *Tenacity* throughout our lives. We ended our journey recommending *Enthusiasm* throughout the entire *InCentivE$* for CREATEing our way process, and we challenged you, our next generation, to begin an *ICE* age in America!

PART 3:

Bringing it Home

EPILOGUE:

My Rescue

When I entered the water after elatedly discovering I was still alive, I continued from memory with my post-ejection checklist. We're trained to ensure that the parachute released from our survival harness, so the wind doesn't drag us under the sea and drown us. Our excellent military land and sea survival training instinctively kicked in. The SEAWARS (Seawater Activated Release System) riser buckles worked as they were designed to, and the chute had already released. It was so dark; I may as well have been blindfolded. I couldn't see my hand held up in front of my face. The January Gulf waters were a chilly 65 degrees as I started sweeping around underneath and around my legs in search of the lifeline attached to my survival equipment and raft. It didn't take long to feel the line, and I grabbed hold of it and pulled the raft to me, hand over hand, until it bumped up against my Life Preserver Unit (LPU). I quickly searched for the side of the raft containing the large metal CO_2 inflation bottle, so I wouldn't get hit on the head, and then I shimmied into the one-man raft. My years as a competition swimmer and squadron life support officer provided familiarity with the equipment and made me pretty comfortable. Regardless, the darkness, wind (15 gusting to 20), waves (6–8 ft. sea states), and chilly water complicated everything. In the raft, I began feeling around for the lines tied off to my survival gear. About the same time, a boat's deck lights began blinking into view between the periodic wave heights obscuring it off the horizon. I clamored around for the survival kit. I could see the glowing green dot of the survival beacon's LED light under the several inches of water in my raft. I chose to leave it alone momentarily to focus on what appeared to be a shrimping boat close to my position. And soon I could see, it was definitely a shrimping boat, given away by the telltale bright spotlighting of the outriggers, dragging the large shrimping nets behind. The boat had all my attention now, so I decided to keep my emergency beacon going, without making radio contact with my wingmen. I didn't want to lose this opportunity to get rescued. Opening up my survival kit, I began a blind feel of each object in the pack, one by one, feeling for the pen flares to shoot toward the boat. Since we are a combat unit, there are no automatic lighting sources attached to our LPUs like the automatic strobe blinkers on airline personal flotation devices, as demonstrated on every flight by safety-trained flight attendants. On the contrary, we wouldn't want to be visible to the enemy after entering the water. I came across the cold-weather hat and gloves during my search and immediately discarded my helmet and donned the hat. Hypothermia had already begun setting in, and I was shaking uncontrollably. I found the pen and the bandolier of flares within a couple minutes, setting them up and electing to dispense no more than four from my limited supply for this rescue attempt. I prepped the night end of my day/night ground flare by feeling the bumps on the plastic caps covering the initiator, careful to then place the items back into the survival kit bag so I could keep the inventory and get to them later if needed. Battling the wind and waves was a constant paddling contest to stay oriented toward the boat for a flare shot toward the bow of the ship. I estimated that my first shot was from about 500 yards away. Fire one! I loaded the next flare and waited for a response from the shrimp boat. He adjusted course. It's working. I watched as he closed the distance but began falling off to my right showing his starboard side. I fired off a second flare. Again, the shrimper course-corrected to starboard bow on. Each time the flare dimmed out, the boat began falling off to port, exposing his starboard side. I loaded a third flare, with the boat now within 100–200 yards. After I fired the third flare, the captain again adjusted course, bearing down on me. I prepped the night flare as I began to see the boat's deckhands rapidly taking in the shrimp net and coming within 50–75 yards of my position. The deck lights reflected off the ocean, providing my first source of light. I lit the night end of my flare, holding it high as I could as the boat started moving from my left to right, his starboard broadside not more than 50 yards away. I could see the deckhand frantically pulling in the net. "They don't see my flare!" I thought the deck lights drowned out the visual of the flare as the boat slipped past to my right. I dipped the end of the flare in the water and tucked it in close to my chest for some welcome heat. "Well, that stinks." Time to move on to my wingmen above. I turned off my beacon, switched to radio and transmitted on guard frequency: "Mayday, Mayday, Mayday, Shark 22, I'm in the water, I'm OK." Twelve uncomfortable minutes had passed since my flight lead and Mako 11 had called for a "Knock It Off" of our fight above, knowing something had gone terribly wrong with Shark 21's wingman. They were well into my search-and-rescue effort when I transmitted on guard. We switched over to our rescue frequency and they got busy finding me beneath the cloud cover above. I was able to hear them circling above, as they had already marked my general location. Mako 13, under the direction of Mako 11 now in charge of my rescue, bravely flew north, looking for a break in the cloud cover, and then safely descended below the cloud deck to circle back and isolate my position. They informed me when they had found an opening and were now below the deck with a visual of the water below. I listened for the sound of their jet noise. I couldn't tell them whether the sound I was hearing was to my east, west, north, or south; I hadn't had a chance to unpack the portable GPS or compass. I had one hand in the water, paddling to stay in rhythm with the wave motion to keep from feeling like I was going to tip over. All I could handle at the moment was the radio or the flares, having to give up one for the other. I fired off a flare, hearing the jet noise while my wingmen started flying a sweeping pattern below the clouds. My wingmen did not call "visual" on the flare. We had a "sound getting further away," "getting closer" jet noise exchange for a bit. I started to hear the sound getting louder from my left ear at one point, so I paddled to square up the sound to my face, trying to equalize the sound between my left and right ears, and I picked up red lights in the distance. I was to their left, since red light is on the left wing. I fired off a pen flare and then started giving them commands to start left turn and stop turn as soon as I saw the red (left wing) and green (right wing) lights equally spaced. I course-corrected them from there until I gave them a countdown to mark my position as they flew over me. "3, 2, 1—mark." They had my position but couldn't see me visually. Mako 13 reminded me to get out my strobe light and turn it on. I'd been so busy with the flares and the radio, I hadn't even gotten to the most visible item in my survival pack. I just hadn't had a minute to consider it until now. Regardless, I couldn't get the snap on the harness pouch for the strobe light undone; the cold water had constricted the metal snap. My manual dexterity and the awkward positioning of the pocket containing the strobe made it impossible to unsnap. I therefore made the risky decision to take off the harness and LPU (flotation) impeding my agility so I could cut the pouch open. This is the first time I thought about sharks. This would not be a good time to cut myself in the dark or poke a hole in the raft without being harnessed to my flotation. Not everything was going according to the textbook, but I was willing to take risks to secure an expeditious recovery; with eight to ten hours of dark and twelve or more until warm sunshine, it was going to be a challenging evening. The closest Coast Guard cutter was reportedly seven hours out, and the Coast Guard helicopter out of Opa-Locka was four hours away, requiring a fuel stop in Marathon to make the journey. I would need to be careful cutting out this strobe light. Like a sea otter, I placed the harness on my chest while feeling for the seam of the pouch. I carefully opened the switchblade knife I kept in my flight suit's right front breast pocket. I flattened myself in the raft to lower my center of gravity and minimize the chance of tipping in the waves. Now it was time to focus on feeling along the seam and cutting out the strobe light. I informed my wingmen I'd be off comm while working on the problem, as they were trying to keep me updated on the Coast Guard cutter and helicopter status. Radio chatter started coming in about an opportunity for pickup by Navy rescue out of Key West. I finished cutting away access to the strobe and fired it up by feel from training memory in the dark. Mako 13 came back almost immediately indicating "Shark 22, we got the strobe, Navy Seahawk helicopter is 60 miles out." Doing some quick math, knowing the max speed of a Seahawk is about 160 knots, and slowing down as they approached my coordinates would be twenty to thirty minutes. The countdown started around ten miles out, and I held the strobe as high as I could for max visibility. I started hearing chopper noise about a mile out, and so I moved the strobe back and forth with the chopper coming into view, serpentining left to right. Mako 13 instructed me to hold the strobe steady and high, as the chopper was losing visual on the strobe due to low ingress and wave heights; when he got close enough, line of sight was no longer an issue. The prop wash and noise overhead were turbulent and deafening. We've been here and done this in survival training. I still hadn't been able to don my harness and life vest after removing it. It became entangled in the lines and gear tied to the raft, and it was too difficult for me to orient and sort out in the dark. I didn't want to risk getting tangled up in the lines as the rescue swimmer was lowered, mask aglow. My G-suit was inflated enough for flotation, and I'm a pretty good swimmer, so I accepted the risk of no LPUs. I knew we would be popping the raft and sinking all the equipment free of lines before getting into the chopper. We don't want any of the gear sucked up or blown into the rotors during extract. My rescue diver swam up and said "Evening, sir, you OK?" "I'm great, now that you're here. Just a bit cold, and muscles starting to cramp." I had to negotiate with him on no LPUs. I convinced him of my swimming ability, that just the inflated G-suit was enough as the equipment was too tangled in the harness, and I didn't have the dexterity to free it up. He relented as I exited the raft and held onto the strap on the back of his harness. He had to carefully ensure to sweep all tied-off equipment into the center of the raft, wrap it in the spray shield, and cut it open to deflate and sink it. There went my helmet and harness.

The next challenge was getting into the chopper. The wind and waves made this extremely difficult, as the lifeline tethered to the chopper slackened and tensed while my rescue swimmer tried to strap me to the straight-back gurney used for ejection survivors (precautions against possible neck and spine injury). He tried to strap my legs, taking away my propulsion above the water line and requiring my arms to work frantically to keep from intaking salt water. Now the lifeline was whipping me in the face, impossible to see and avoid. After strapping my legs, he said, "Sir, I need to strap your arms now." "Not gonna happen," I said. "I'm gonna drown without my arms keeping me above, just tell them to pull it up and I'll hang on." "Sir, I can't . . ." "Just do it! I'm not gonna be able to take on much more seawater, and I'm cramping up." He gave the signal and up I went. The medics looked me over and did their best to cover me up and get me warm. We landed at Key West Hospital shortly after pickup and I was transported inside.

Key West Hospital took good care of me, warming me up in heat blankets and ensuring I had no severe neck or spinal injuries before allowing me to go home. I now had time to review the events in my head and try to make sense of what had happened. Not everything had gone training-textbook, since I recognized I was spatially disoriented till getting picked up by our Navy buddies. The critics would probably have a field day during the safety and accident investigation board, but none of that mattered as I did my best to survive, given the unfortunate circumstances I had gotten myself into.

I would discover later that there was some divine intervention and good luck in play when the rescue helicopter crew captured the image of an unlit, abandoned Air Combat Maneuvering Instrumentation (ACMI) metal tower structure outside the cockpit canopy during their debrief and tape review. The tower was dangerously close to the rotors. Focused on us below, they never saw it. Survivor's guilt would have been extremely hard to live with if they'd perished rescuing me. And remember the shrimp boat I encountered when I initially entered the water? Turns out they were so close to my position their shrimp nets swept up my ejection seat as they slipped by. My actual ejection seat was ceremoniously delivered to me after being turned into a desk chair by the professional non-commissioned officers and airmen who maintain our squadron's jets and equipment. My wing commander graciously sought and approved for the ejection seat release into my custody and it now sits in my home as a constant source of gratitude.

Everything worked out. I got a little beat up during the ejection, with some minor neck, back disc compression, and torn knee ligaments. I got a little beat up by the investigators as well. I didn't disagree with the criticism. I got over it, keeping my "$en¢e of humor" about the event. We called it "the night Stink went in the drink," and I've endured a lot of ribbing from my colleagues over my "Satori" experience. You develop pretty thick skin from spending twenty-eight years amongst an opinionated group of warriors always training to win. My accident, though preventable, was part of the "probable" dangers of training to be lethal, so I was forgiven. Overall, I received incredible support from my leadership and colleagues getting off DNIF (Duty Not Including Flying) thirty-eight days later. My operations officer at the time, warrior that he is, had me back in the saddle flying my very first mission, at night, over the water, with my friend as an instructor observer, ensuring I got the wiggles out. Nine years after my accident, I would be forced to retire with twenty-eight years of service, flying my last 4-vs.-4 training mission "fini" flight at 50 years old. An emotional day to be thankful for the people, the mission, and the flying I was so privileged to enjoy for so long.

Thank you all: you know who you are!

NEAR DEATH EXPERIENCE
(NDE) testimony

Those who became aware of my accident through word of mouth inevitably asked if coming so close to death changed my life in any way. The most common questions were about the fear of sharks while in the water, post-traumatic stress disorder (PTSD), or a spiritual awakening.

The aviator business has varying degrees of low to high risk, depending on the type of aircraft and mission we're involved with. Employing fighter aircraft weapon systems is in the high-risk category, so I believe most fighter pilots are already conditioned to the finality of gross errors and "not our day" moments in the air-to-air and air-to-ground arenas. Training and the ejection seat are our confidants, despite our awareness of today's warfare technological "target the pilot" advances in modern missile development. Pilots have undergone years of training, testing, and evaluating by the time we're allowed to operate weapon systems. We aren't straight out of high school with several months of training, asked to knock down doors in Iraq or Afghanistan; it's a completely different environment for risk and stress. Accepting the risks, thrills, dangers, and persistent training of our profession conditions us against PTSD. Few of us have not experienced a close call, with a debrief to talk about it and instructionally fix it before heading to the bar to shake it off with a few laughs and rolling of the dice, "4-5-what?". The details of our events, however, are permanently ingrained. When asked about my experience, I can still see the event sequence, the instruments, my head and hand movements, outside visuals, and environment conditions, down to the orange flame from the rocket boost of the ejection seat and the chilly startle as I entered the water. I can hear the high-speed apparent wind noise hum from outside the canopy when I first felt something wasn't right. I can smell the sea air, taste the sea spray, and feel the constant shiver of my body struggling to stay warm. Yes, all the details are still imprinted, but not in a negative or dysfunctional way. I'm enjoying and living a fulfilling life today. I didn't have any dramatic spiritual visions, but I do have some personal takeaways that have become firmly cemented in my life approach and habitual behavior in the twelve years since.

"Does your life really flash before your eyes?" Yes. My final movie reel moments were scenes from the most important relationships in my life—my family. There were no scenes in the realm of achievement, success, or material importance except for the brief, conscious thought of being glad I had purchased higher life insurance for my wife and kids. There was a brief moment of "I'm too fast to eject, so ride it in, ending the stress at home," quickly replaced with an "I'm not letting anyone else raise my kids" will to survive. Thoughts of letting my leadership down, poorly reflecting on our squadron, and "there goes my career" outcomes whizzed by but were quickly replaced by my awareness that I had given everything, 100 percent of my "Fighter Pilot 101" best. The human brain becomes a supercomputer fueled by adrenaline shock to the amygdala as life scenes play in the background together with the effort to solve the problem and make life-saving decisions. Too fast for a 6,000-feet-above-sea-level ejection made 2,000-feet altitude my limit for solving this particular problem, leaving my fate to the ejection seat if not successful in the short time I had left. I was mindful of leading the lag of the altimeter a bit. When I reached for and pulled the ejection handle, the 0.18 second canopy separation seat initiator delay against a rapidly unwinding altimeter made me feel that I had waited too long. My body relaxed, anticipating impact, and my mind temporally distorted time in a *Matrix*-like slow-motion. I was super-aware—a "Satori" experience, if you like. I can still see the airspeed and altitude numbers passing on the dials just before being obscured by orange light. I can hear the distinct popping of the canopy bolts and the air rush noise and feel the 12 g compression in the seat as my body snapped uncontrollably to the will of the 400-mph apparent wind. I had assumed the violence was me and the jet impacting the water. There was no light to illuminate the experience. There was a sense of peace, calm, and transcendence as the movie reel fast-forwarded from beginning to a projected end. The first law of thermodynamics states energy can neither be created nor destroyed—it can only be transformed. I think the best way to paint the picture of this transcendent experience for my reader is to imagine once we release control and turn over our life to the universe anticipating our impending death—the gaps in our lives get filled in spiritually before transforming materially into energy (fish food) for the sea. From playing in a puddle with my little brother in the driveway of our first home in Florida to the vision of my kids throwing their graduation caps in the air and my wife bouncing our unborn grandkid on her knee. It was a spiritual, slow-motion transition from life to death. That feeling I experienced has made me comfortable with death. It was peaceful and euphoric, with nothing to fear.

Did I become a changed man? In subtle ways I am, but nothing dramatic. There was an adjustment period. Our Military OneSource program was an amazing resource for my wife and me. I'm the same person I was before, with a bit more pep in my step, enjoying the time I have left to positively impact my family, myself, and others. I'm more tolerant and patient, I talk less, I listen and laugh more. I've replaced previous FOMO sentiments with JOMO (Joy of Missing Out) acceptance. The experience made me more deliberate in my decision-making. I'm open and considerate toward others' input but have lowered my attachment to what others may think of me or my decisions, except for the concerns of my wife and children. I've become more mindful of caring for myself physically, mentally, and spiritually, extending my time as long as healthfully possible. Money thoughts are oriented around its exchange for more time to experience the things I enjoy doing the most with the people I love the most. Over it all, I'm grateful to be alive, witnessing the wonder surrounding us.

Thanks for spending this time with me. I encourage all readers to post your "been there, done that" stories on my website, <u>combatstinkythinking.com,</u> so other young adults creating their way can learn from our experiences. I encourage suggestions and comments for blog discussion. It's been a fun journey sharing these thoughts with you, and I look forward to hearing yours.

Here's to you CREATEing your way, and the beginning of an *ICE* age!

ACKNOWLEDGMENTS

I am indebted to the men and women of our United States military forces, especially those airman, civilians, instructors, colleagues, wingmen, and peers with whom I served and who set the example that helped me create my way. To my beautiful wife, Terri, for her love, patience, and input while writing this book, and for grinning, bearing with everything, and staying positive throughout the challenges of raising four children while serving. To my children Erika, Dean, Cole and Jessica who add joy and purpose to my days. Thank you to my brother for his continued servant leadership and my parents and extended family for all their support. As a first-time author, I want to thank Neil R. Coulter for his superb mentoring, guidance, and editorial services in writing this book. Thank you to my former commander Rob "Mumbles" Polumbo, Major General (ret) USAF, for his continued leadership example and connecting me to Neil. Shout out to one of my wingmen, C. W. Lemoine, a prolific author himself, for his encouragement and shared experience writing books. Thank you to my friend Marshall Carey, my spiritual journey bud and invaluable objective resource for improving this work. Heartfelt gratitude goes to my chain of command, colleagues, wingmen and friends for their unwavering support and confidence in me before, during and after my accident. Finally, my sincere thanks to Courtney "Rosco" Collier for his leadership during our years serving together and for coordinating the efforts of numerous wingmen, airmen, and agencies bringing me home to my family on January 15, 2008.

WORKS CITED

Hawley, Jack, *The Bhagavad Gita: A Walkthrough for Westerners*. New World Library, 2001

APPENDIX

The Mentor-Mentee Matrix

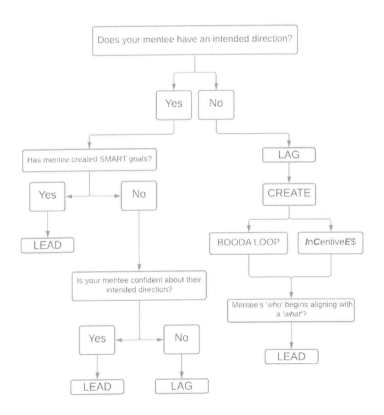

LEAD *pursuit course:*

- Learn about mentee's interest and explore it together
- Engage 'been there, done that' resources
- Assess courses of action
- Direct experientially

LAG *pursuit course:*

- Listen to mentee's story and evaluate their uncertainties, doubts or imperfect thinking
- Advise mentee how to use the CREATE checklist, exercise the BOODA loop and develop *InCentivE$*
- Guide the mentee in transition to a LEAD pursuit course

What are **SMART** *goals?*

- Specific
- Measurable
- Attainable
- Relevant
- Time-based